COINS to CROWNS

A Journey to Financial Empowerment

SMITH E. HECTOR

Copyright

Preface

Welcome to "Coins to Crowns: A Journey to Financial Empowerment." In the pursuit of financial well-being, this book serves as a compass, guiding you through the transformative path from managing coins to wearing the crowns of financial empowerment. It is an exploration of principles, strategies, and a mindset that not only empowers your present but also shapes a legacy for the future.

The Journey Unveiled

Embarking on the journey to financial empowerment is akin to setting sail on uncharted waters. It's a journey filled with discoveries, challenges, and triumphs. As we navigate this voyage together, the pages ahead unfold a roadmap—a comprehensive guide designed to empower you with the knowledge, tools, and inspiration needed to achieve sustained financial success.

Purposeful Wealth Building

At the heart of this journey lies the concept of purposeful wealth building. It's not just about accumulating riches; it's about defining a purpose that resonates with your values and aspirations. As you delve into these pages, consider the "why" behind your financial goals. This purpose will be the driving force propelling you forward when the seas get rough.

Generational Empowerment

Financial empowerment is not an isolated endeavor—it's a legacy that transcends generations. This book underscores the importance of inclusivity, involving family members in the financial discourse. The principles discussed are not mere tools for personal prosperity; they are foundations for a collective legacy of financial empowerment that echoes through the corridors of time.

Education as the Cornerstone

At the cornerstone of this journey is education. Financial literacy is the key that unlocks the doors to informed decision-making. Whether you're well-versed in financial concepts or just starting, these pages offer insights into budgeting, investing, debt management, and more. Think of this book as your personalized financial classroom, equipping you with the knowledge to navigate the complex terrain of personal finance.

Strategic Goal Setting

Setting realistic and achievable goals is a fundamental step toward financial empowerment. The chapters ahead guide you in crafting goals that align with your vision, breaking them down into manageable steps. Through strategic goal setting, you gain clarity, motivation, and a sense of direction—essential elements for a successful financial journey.

Budgeting Wisdom

Budgeting is not a restraint but a liberating tool. It provides a roadmap for your financial resources, allowing you to allocate funds to your priorities. Dive into the budgeting techniques presented here, and discover how this practice transforms your financial landscape, paving the way for intentional and purposeful spending.

Emergency Fund Essentials

Building a financial fortress against unexpected storms is a cornerstone of financial empowerment. Learn the essentials of creating and maintaining an emergency fund—a safety net that ensures your journey isn't derailed by unforeseen circumstances. It's a shield that provides both financial security and peace of mind.

The Crucial Role of Financial Literacy

In a world of evolving financial landscapes, literacy becomes a compass. The importance of financial literacy cannot be overstated. These pages unravel the significance of understanding economic principles, investment strategies, and the language of finance. A literate navigator is a confident one, and confidence is the fuel for financial empowerment.

Diversifying Income Streams

Exploring additional income streams is not just a strategy; it's a mindset. The concept of diversified income is a gateway to financial resilience and independence. Here, we delve into entrepreneurial ventures, investment opportunities, and ways to expand your financial horizons. It's about unlocking the potential of your skills and resources.

Cultivating an Entrepreneurial Mindset

Beyond the pursuit of traditional income lies the entrepreneurial mindset—an approach that sees challenges as opportunities and values innovation. These chapters explore the principles of entrepreneurship, offering insights into risk-taking, creative thinking, and cultivating resilience—a mindset that propels you toward financial autonomy.

Understanding and Managing Debts

Debt, when understood and managed strategically, can be a tool for wealth creation. Unpack the layers of different types of debts, discerning between those that hinder and those that propel your financial goals. Navigate the landscape of responsible borrowing and debt reduction strategies, reclaiming control over your financial narrative.

Savings Mindset Cultivation

In the heart of financial empowerment lies the cultivation of a savings mindset. Beyond saving for specific goals, it's about adopting a lifestyle that values financial prudence. Explore the art of mindful saving, understanding that each dollar saved is a step closer to financial freedom and security.

Effective Saving Habits and Techniques

Saving is not just about putting money aside; it's about optimizing your resources. These pages delve into effective saving habits and techniques that align with your financial goals. From automating savings to exploring high-yield accounts, discover ways to make your money work for you.

Introduction to Various Investment Options

Venture into the realm of investments, where each choice is a step toward wealth creation. This section introduces various investment options, from traditional avenues like stocks and bonds to newer concepts like cryptocurrencies. It's an exploration that empowers you to make informed decisions aligned with your risk tolerance and financial goals.

Creating an Investment Portfolio

Building an investment portfolio is an art—a strategic composition of assets that aligns with your financial objectives. Navigate through the principles of diversification, risk assessment, and long-term investing. Craft a portfolio that not only withstands market fluctuations but propels you toward financial growth.

Risk Assessment in Financial Decisions

Risk is inherent in financial decisions, but with knowledge comes the power to assess and manage it. These pages guide you through the intricacies of risk assessment, empowering you to make informed decisions that balance potential returns with your comfort level. It's about understanding risk, not fearing it.

Mitigating and Managing Financial Risks

Beyond assessment lies mitigation and management. Explore strategies to mitigate financial risks, whether in investments, entrepreneurship, or unexpected life events. A prepared navigator is a resilient one, ready to navigate financial challenges with poise and strategic acumen.

Celebrating Small Victories

In the journey to financial empowerment, every milestone, no matter how small, is a victory worth celebrating. These chapters explore the significance of acknowledging and rejoicing in your achievements. It's about fostering a positive relationship with your financial journey, building momentum for sustained success.

Tracking Progress Toward Financial Goals

Progress tracking is the compass that ensures you're on the right course. Uncover the tools and techniques to monitor your financial goals, adapting strategies as needed. It's about staying attuned to your journey, making informed decisions, and enjoying the satisfaction of progress.

Passing on Financial Knowledge

In the spirit of empowerment, these chapters delve into the importance of passing on financial knowledge. Whether to family members, friends, or the community, sharing insights becomes a legacy—a contribution that ripples through generations, inspiring others to embark on their financial journeys.

Creating a Legacy of Financial Empowerment

Financial empowerment is not just a personal achievement; it's a legacy that shapes the financial landscape for generations to come. The concluding chapters explore how to create a legacy of financial empowerment—building a foundation that stands as a beacon of inspiration and guidance.

Recap of Key Concepts

As you embark on this journey, a recap of key concepts provides a compass—a synthesis of principles that underscore the holistic approach to financial empowerment. It's a reminder of the pillars that sustain your financial journey, ensuring you navigate with purpose and resilience.

Encouragement for Sustained Financial Empowerment

Finally, find words of encouragement that echo through these pages, a reminder that sustained financial empowerment is not just a destination but a way of life. It's an invitation to stay motivated, resilient, and committed to the principles that shape your financial legacy.

Welcome to "Coins to Crowns: A Journey to Financial Empowerment." May this book be your guide, mentor, and companion on the transformative odyssey toward financial well-being. May it empower you to not only manage your coins but to wear the crowns of lasting financial success.

Let the journey begin.

Dedication

To the dreamers and the planners,
the savers and the risk-takers,
To those who navigate the seas of coins
with dreams of crowns on distant horizons.

This book is dedicated to you—
the curious minds and courageous hearts
embarking on the journey of financial
empowerment.

May these pages be your compass,
guiding you through the landscapes of budgeting,
investing, and the art of saving wisely.

In your pursuit of coins turning into crowns,
may you find inspiration, knowledge, and resilience.

Here's to the readers—
the architects of their financial destinies,
May your journey be prosperous,
your goals attainable,
and your crowns worn with pride.

For in every page turned,
lies the potential for a brighter financial future.

With unwavering dedication,

Smith E. Hector

Table of Contents

INTRODUCTION

"Coins to Crowns: A Journey to Financial Empowerment" is a comprehensive guide designed to empower individuals on their path to financial independence. This book aims to demystify the world of personal finance and provide practical insights, tools, and strategies to help readers transform their financial lives.

In the introductory section, readers are introduced to the overarching purpose of the book—to guide them on a transformative journey from managing mere coins to attaining the metaphorical crowns of financial success and empowerment. The importance of financial empowerment is emphasized, highlighting how it transcends mere monetary accumulation and contributes to a sense of security, freedom, and fulfillment.

The initial chapters focus on establishing a solid foundation. Chapter 1 encourages readers to assess their current financial situation honestly. By providing practical frameworks, readers learn how to set realistic financial goals tailored to their unique circumstances. This introspective approach sets the stage for the subsequent chapters, creating a roadmap for readers to follow.

Chapter 2 delves into the essential elements of building a solid financial foundation. Budgeting techniques are introduced, allowing readers to gain control over their finances and allocate resources effectively. The importance of establishing an emergency fund is emphasized, serving as a financial safety net during unexpected circumstances. Together, these chapters lay the groundwork for financial stability and resilience.

Recognizing the pivotal role of knowledge in financial empowerment, Chapter 3 focuses on investing in education. The significance of financial literacy is explored, and readers are guided towards accessible educational resources and tools. By investing in their knowledge base, readers are equipped to make informed decisions, navigate complex financial landscapes, and adapt to evolving economic conditions.

"Coins to Crowns" then shifts its focus to expanding income streams in Chapter 4. Readers are encouraged to explore opportunities beyond traditional employment, fostering an entrepreneurial mindset. This chapter provides insights into various income-generating avenues, empowering readers to diversify their sources of revenue and increase their financial resilience.

Chapter 5 addresses the challenge of managing debts strategically. Readers gain an understanding of different types of debts and are introduced to effective debt reduction strategies. By mastering the art of debt management, readers can alleviate financial burdens and redirect resources towards wealth-building initiatives.

The transformative power of saving is explored in Chapter 6. Readers learn to cultivate a savings mindset and adopt effective saving habits. Practical techniques are shared to help readers build a financial cushion, providing both security and flexibility in pursuing their financial goals.

Moving into the realm of investments, Chapter 7 introduces readers to various investment options. From traditional investments like stocks and bonds to alternative avenues such as real estate and

entrepreneurship, readers gain insights into creating
a diversified investment portfolio. This chapter
serves as a guide for making informed investment
decisions aligned with individual risk tolerance and
financial goals.

Chapter 8 navigates the complexities of risk.
Readers are educated on the importance of risk
assessment in financial decision-making and
provided with strategies to mitigate and manage
risks effectively. Understanding and navigating risks
are essential components of achieving sustained
financial success.

Chapter 9 celebrates milestones on the journey to
financial independence. Readers are encouraged to
acknowledge and appreciate small victories,
fostering a positive and motivated mindset. Tracking
progress towards financial goals becomes a source
of inspiration and reinforcement for continued
efforts.

The final substantive chapter, Chapter 10, explores
the concept of generational wealth. Readers are
prompted to consider the broader impact of their
financial decisions on future generations. By

imparting financial knowledge and creating a legacy of financial empowerment, individuals contribute to a lasting impact on their families and communities.

The conclusion of the book recaps key concepts, reinforcing the transformative journey outlined in "Coins to Crowns." The reader is left with a sense of accomplishment, armed with newfound knowledge and practical tools to navigate their ongoing financial journey.

In addition to the main content, the book includes appendices with additional resources, further reading recommendations, and practical worksheets. These resources enhance the book's practical application, providing readers with tangible tools to implement the strategies outlined throughout the chapters.

In essence, "Coins to Crowns: A Journey to Financial Empowerment" is more than a guide to managing money; it is a roadmap to personal and financial transformation. Through a blend of practical advice, motivational insights, and actionable strategies, this book empowers individuals to take control of their financial destinies, guiding them from the realm of coins to the attainment of their metaphorical crowns.

Financial empowerment is a transformative concept that transcends the mere accumulation of wealth; it is a dynamic force that empowers individuals to take control of their financial destinies, leading to a life characterized by security, freedom, and fulfillment. In a world where economic uncertainties and financial challenges abound, the importance of financial empowerment cannot be overstated.

At its core, financial empowerment is about giving individuals the tools, knowledge, and confidence to make informed and effective decisions about their money. It enables people to navigate the complexities of personal finance, from budgeting and saving to investing and managing debts. The significance of financial empowerment extends beyond individual well-being; it ripples through communities and society at large, contributing to economic resilience and stability.

One of the fundamental aspects of financial empowerment is the ability to set and achieve realistic financial goals. When individuals have a clear understanding of their financial situation and a vision for their future, they can chart a course toward economic success. Whether the goal is to buy a home, start a business, or retire comfortably, financial empowerment provides the framework for turning aspirations into achievable milestones.

Moreover, financial empowerment fosters a sense of security. An individual equipped with financial knowledge is better prepared to handle unexpected challenges such as medical emergencies, job loss, or economic downturns. Building an emergency fund, a key component of financial empowerment, acts as a financial safety net, providing a buffer against unforeseen circumstances and reducing the stress associated with financial instability.

Financial empowerment is also a catalyst for freedom. It liberates individuals from the constraints of financial dependence, allowing them to make choices based on their aspirations rather than financial limitations. Whether it's pursuing higher education, starting a business, or taking a career risk, financial empowerment provides the flexibility and resources to explore opportunities and realize one's full potential.

The ability to generate income beyond traditional employment is a crucial aspect of financial empowerment. Diversifying income streams, exploring entrepreneurial ventures, and embracing a mindset of financial abundance are key components of this empowerment. By expanding income sources, individuals not only increase their earning potential but also enhance their resilience in the face of economic uncertainties.

In addition to financial security and freedom, financial empowerment plays a pivotal role in long-term wealth creation. Through prudent budgeting, strategic debt management, and informed investment decisions, individuals can build a solid financial foundation and work towards achieving their wealth-building goals. This not only secures their future but also opens avenues for generational wealth, creating a lasting impact on the well-being of future generations.

Financial empowerment is closely tied to the concept of financial literacy. Knowledge about money management, investment strategies, and understanding economic principles equips individuals with the tools needed to navigate the ever-changing financial landscape. A financially literate population is better positioned to make informed decisions, resist financial exploitation, and contribute to a more economically resilient society.

Furthermore, financial empowerment fosters a mindset shift from passive consumerism to active financial participation. Instead of being mere recipients of financial products and services, empowered individuals actively engage with their finances, making intentional choices that align with their goals. This shift in mindset is transformative, as it encourages individuals to take ownership of their financial well-being rather than relying solely on external factors.

The impact of financial empowerment is not limited to individual lives; it extends to communities and society as a whole. Empowered individuals are more likely to contribute to their local economies, support community initiatives, and participate in activities that promote economic growth. In this way, financial empowerment becomes a catalyst for broader societal progress and prosperity.

Moreover, addressing financial disparities and promoting inclusivity are critical aspects of financial empowerment. By providing equal access to financial education and resources, societies can work towards narrowing the wealth gap and ensuring that everyone has the opportunity to thrive economically. Financial empowerment, therefore, becomes a powerful tool for promoting social justice and equality.

In conclusion, the importance of financial empowerment cannot be overstated in the context of today's dynamic and often unpredictable economic landscape. It is a catalyst for personal growth, a shield against financial uncertainties, and a driver of societal progress. By providing individuals with the knowledge, tools, and mindset needed to take control of their financial destinies, financial empowerment sets the stage for a future characterized by security, freedom, and fulfillment. As we recognize the transformative power of financial empowerment, we pave the way for a more resilient, inclusive, and economically vibrant society.

CHAPTER 1: The Starting Point

Assessing your current financial situation is a crucial first step on the journey to financial empowerment. It involves a comprehensive examination of your income, expenses, assets, and liabilities to gain a clear understanding of where you stand financially. This process not only provides a snapshot of your current financial health but also serves as the foundation for setting realistic goals and making informed financial decisions.

To begin the assessment, start with a detailed analysis of your income. This includes your primary source of income, such as your salary or business earnings, as well as any additional sources of income, such as rental income or dividends. Understanding the stability and consistency of your income streams is essential, as it forms the basis for budgeting and future financial planning.

Next, scrutinize your expenses meticulously. Categorize your spending into fixed and variable expenses. Fixed expenses include essential costs that remain relatively constant, such as mortgage or rent payments, utilities, insurance, and loan repayments. Variable expenses, on the other hand, fluctuate based on your discretionary spending, including groceries, dining out, entertainment, and other non-essential items.

Creating a detailed budget is a powerful tool for assessing your spending habits. Compare your actual expenses against your budget to identify areas where you may be overspending or where adjustments can be made. This process not only sheds light on your financial habits but also helps in allocating resources more effectively towards your financial goals.

Simultaneously, evaluate your debt situation. List all outstanding debts, including credit cards, loans, and any other financial obligations. Take note of the interest rates, outstanding balances, and monthly repayment amounts. Understanding your debt landscape is crucial for developing a strategy to manage and, if necessary, reduce your debt burden.

An essential aspect of assessing your financial situation is determining your net worth. This involves subtracting your total liabilities from your total assets. Assets may include savings, investments, real estate, and other valuable possessions, while liabilities encompass debts and financial obligations. A positive net worth indicates that your assets exceed your liabilities, reflecting a healthy financial position.

Consider your savings and emergency fund. Savings act as a financial cushion and provide the flexibility to navigate unexpected expenses or income fluctuations. Evaluate the adequacy of your savings relative to your financial goals and potential emergencies. If your emergency fund is insufficient, prioritizing its growth becomes a crucial part of your financial strategy.

Review your investment portfolio, if applicable. Assess the performance of your investments and consider whether they align with your financial goals and risk tolerance. Diversification, or spreading investments across different asset classes, is a key principle in managing risk and optimizing returns.

Insurance coverage is another integral component of your financial health. Evaluate your insurance policies, including health, life, auto, and property insurance. Ensure that your coverage meets your current needs and consider whether adjustments or additional coverage are necessary.

As you assess your financial situation, it's crucial to consider your financial goals. Are you saving for a home, planning for education, or preparing for retirement? Clearly defined goals provide direction and purpose to your financial decisions. Evaluate the progress you've made towards achieving these goals and adjust your strategies if needed.

Consider the economic environment and potential external factors that may impact your finances. Changes in interest rates, inflation, or job market conditions can influence your financial stability. Being aware of these factors allows you to proactively adapt your financial strategies to navigate changing circumstances.

Now that you have a comprehensive overview of your financial situation, it's time to reflect on your financial mindset and behavior. Assess your attitudes towards money, spending habits, and overall financial philosophy. Recognizing any negative patterns or beliefs is essential for cultivating a positive and empowering relationship with your finances.

The assessment process is not a one-time endeavor; it should be revisited periodically to ensure that your financial strategies align with your evolving goals and circumstances. Life changes, such as job transitions, marriage, or the birth of a child, can impact your financial situation, necessitating adjustments to your financial plan.

In summary, assessing your current financial situation is a holistic process that involves examining your income, expenses, debts, assets, and overall financial well-being. This introspective analysis provides a foundation for informed decision-making, goal setting, and the development of effective financial strategies. Regularly revisiting this assessment ensures that your financial plan remains dynamic and responsive to the ever-changing landscape of your life and the broader economic environment. Ultimately, the goal of this assessment is to empower you to take control of your finances, make informed choices, and embark on a journey towards financial well-being and empowerment.

Setting realistic financial goals is a fundamental step in the journey toward financial empowerment. Well-defined goals provide direction, motivation, and a framework for making informed financial decisions. Whether you aspire to buy a home, pay off debt, save for education, or achieve financial independence, the process of setting realistic financial goals involves careful consideration of your current financial situation, future aspirations, and the steps required to bridge the gap.

Begin by conducting a comprehensive assessment of your current financial landscape, as discussed in the previous response. Understanding your income, expenses, debts, assets, and net worth provides a solid foundation for establishing realistic and achievable financial goals. This introspective analysis serves as the starting point for identifying areas that require improvement and opportunities for growth.

With a clear understanding of your financial situation, embark on a reflection of your life priorities and aspirations. Consider both short-term and long-term objectives, encompassing various aspects of your life, such as career, family, education, and lifestyle. These goals form the basis for your financial plan and should be aligned with your values, aspirations, and overall life vision.

Categorize your financial goals into short-term, medium-term, and long-term objectives. Short-term goals typically span one year or less and may include building an emergency fund, paying off a small debt, or saving for a vacation. Medium-term goals, with a timeframe of two to five years, could involve saving for a down payment on a home, funding higher education, or starting a business. Long-term goals extend beyond five years and often include retirement planning, creating generational wealth, or achieving financial independence.

Once you've identified your financial goals, ensure they are specific, measurable, achievable, relevant, and time-bound (SMART). Specificity provides clarity about what you want to accomplish, measurability enables you to track progress, achievability ensures feasibility, relevance aligns goals with your values, and setting a timeframe adds a sense of urgency and accountability.

For example, rather than setting a vague goal like "save money," a SMART goal would be "save $5,000 in the next 12 months for an emergency fund." This specific, measurable, and time-bound goal provides a clear target and a timeframe for achievement.

Prioritize your goals based on their significance and urgency. This helps in allocating resources and efforts efficiently. For instance, if you have high-interest debt, prioritizing debt repayment might take precedence over other goals to minimize interest costs and improve your overall financial health.

Consider the concept of the "financial pyramid" when setting goals. At the base of the pyramid are essential goals like building an emergency fund and paying off high-interest debt. As you move up the pyramid, goals become more aspirational, such as investing for retirement or funding your children's education. This hierarchical approach ensures a solid financial foundation before pursuing more ambitious objectives.

Understand the financial trade-offs and sacrifices required to achieve your goals. Evaluate the impact of your goals on your daily life and identify areas where adjustments can be made. This process involves distinguishing between needs and wants, making conscious spending choices, and practicing financial discipline to stay on track.

Financial goals are dynamic and may need adjustments over time. Life circumstances, economic conditions, and personal priorities can change, influencing the feasibility or relevance of certain goals. Regularly review and reassess your financial goals to ensure they align with your evolving circumstances and aspirations.

Breaking down larger goals into smaller, actionable steps enhances manageability and provides a roadmap for progress. For instance, if your goal is to save $50,000 for a down payment on a home in five years, break it down into saving $10,000 annually or roughly $834 per month. This approach makes the goal less daunting and allows you to celebrate smaller victories along the way.

Consider seeking professional advice when setting complex financial goals, such as retirement planning or investment strategies. Financial advisors can provide insights, guidance, and expertise to ensure your goals are realistic, tailored to your unique circumstances, and aligned with your risk tolerance.

Collaborate with your partner or family members when setting financial goals that involve shared responsibilities. Open communication ensures everyone is on the same page, contributing to a unified approach and shared commitment towards achieving the established goals.

Celebrate milestones and achievements along the way. Recognizing and rewarding progress reinforces positive financial behavior and motivates continued efforts. Whether it's reaching a savings target, paying off a significant portion of debt, or achieving a career milestone, acknowledging your successes contributes to a positive financial mindset.

Lastly, embrace the concept of flexibility in goal-setting. Life is unpredictable, and unforeseen circumstances may arise. Being adaptable and open to adjustments ensures that you can navigate unexpected challenges while staying focused on your overall financial objectives.

In conclusion, setting realistic financial goals is a dynamic and intentional process that involves aligning your aspirations with your current financial situation. By conducting a thorough assessment, categorizing goals, applying the SMART criteria, and prioritizing objectives, you create a roadmap for financial success. Regular reviews, adaptability, and celebrating achievements contribute to a sustainable and empowering approach to goal-setting. Ultimately, well-defined financial goals not only guide your financial decisions but also serve as a source of motivation and empowerment on your journey to financial well-being.

CHAPTER 2: Building a Solid Foundation

Budgeting is a fundamental financial tool that empowers individuals to take control of their finances, manage spending, and work toward achieving their financial goals. Various budgeting techniques exist, each offering a unique approach to help individuals tailor their budgeting strategy to their specific needs, lifestyle, and financial aspirations. In this exploration, we will delve into several popular budgeting techniques, outlining their principles and discussing how they can be applied to foster financial stability and success.

1. Traditional or Static Budgeting:

The traditional budgeting method involves creating a detailed plan for income and expenses based on historical data. It is often done monthly and is ideal for those with consistent income and relatively stable expenses. Individuals estimate their income and allocate specific amounts to various spending categories, such as housing, transportation, food, and entertainment. This approach provides a clear overview but may lack flexibility for those with irregular incomes or changing expenses.

2. Zero-Based Budgeting:

Zero-based budgeting requires assigning every dollar of income a specific purpose, with the goal of "zeroing out" the budget by allocating all funds to various categories, including savings and debt repayment. This method encourages intentional spending and ensures that every dollar has a designated role, preventing money from sitting idle. Zero-based budgeting is effective for those seeking a proactive approach to managing their finances and minimizing unnecessary expenses.

3. Envelope System:

The envelope system is a cash-based budgeting method. It involves allocating a specific amount of cash to different spending categories and placing the cash in separate envelopes labeled for each category. Once the cash in an envelope is spent, individuals must wait until the next budgeting period to replenish it. This technique is beneficial for curbing overspending and promoting awareness of where money goes, but it requires disciplined cash management.

4. 50/30/20 Budget Rule:

The 50/30/20 budget rule, popularized by Senator Elizabeth Warren, suggests allocating 50% of income to needs, 30% to wants, and 20% to savings and debt repayment. This rule provides a simple and flexible framework for budgeting, allowing individuals to prioritize essentials while still enjoying discretionary spending and saving for the future. It is particularly suitable for those looking for a straightforward guideline to structure their finances.

5. Bi-Weekly Budgeting:

Bi-weekly budgeting aligns with the frequency of many individuals' paychecks. Instead of budgeting on a monthly basis, individuals allocate funds and plan expenses based on a bi-weekly timeframe. This method can be advantageous for those who receive income bi-weekly and find it more convenient to

manage their finances in sync with their pay
schedule.

6. Percentage-Based Budgeting:

Percentage-based budgeting involves allocating a
specific percentage of income to different spending
categories. For example, housing might be allocated
30% of income, while groceries might be allocated
10%. This method provides a flexible framework
that can be adapted to various income levels. It
ensures that essential categories receive appropriate
priority without being overly prescriptive about
specific dollar amounts.

7. Emergency Fund Budgeting:

This budgeting approach focuses on building and
maintaining an emergency fund as a top priority.
Individuals allocate a significant portion of their
income to emergency savings before budgeting for
other categories. This method aims to create a
financial safety net, ensuring individuals have funds
available to cover unexpected expenses or financial
disruptions.

8. Seasonal Budgeting:

Seasonal budgeting recognizes that certain expenses vary throughout the year. For example, heating costs might be higher in winter, and travel expenses might spike during holidays. By anticipating these seasonal fluctuations and budgeting accordingly, individuals can ensure they have the funds needed for specific periods without compromising their overall financial stability.

9. Reverse Budgeting:

Reverse budgeting focuses on saving first and spending what remains. Individuals determine their savings goals and allocate funds to savings and investments as a top priority. The remaining income is then used for living expenses and discretionary spending. This method prioritizes long-term financial goals and ensures that saving is a non-negotiable part of the budget.

10. App-Based Budgeting:

With the advent of technology, various budgeting apps have become popular tools for managing finances. These apps often use algorithms and automation to categorize spending, track income, and provide real-time insights into financial behavior. Examples include Mint, YNAB (You Need A Budget), and PocketGuard. App-based budgeting is particularly appealing to those who prefer digital solutions for tracking and managing their finances on the go.

Implementing Budgeting Techniques:

1. Define Your Financial Goals:
   - Identify short-term, medium-term, and long-term financial goals.
   - Prioritize goals based on urgency, importance, and feasibility.

2. Assess Your Income:
   - Calculate your total monthly income, considering regular and irregular sources.
   - Ensure an accurate understanding of your take-home pay after taxes and deductions.

3. List Your Expenses:
   - Categorize expenses into fixed (e.g., rent, utilities) and variable (e.g., groceries, entertainment).
   - Include discretionary spending categories to capture non-essential expenses.

4. Allocate Funds:
   - Choose a budgeting technique that aligns with your preferences and financial situation.
   - Allocate funds to categories based on the chosen technique, ensuring every dollar has a purpose.

5. Review and Adjust:
   - Regularly review your budget to track spending and ensure alignment with your financial goals.
   - Be open to adjusting your budget based on changes in income, expenses, or financial priorities.

6. Build Emergency Savings:
   - Prioritize building an emergency fund to cover unforeseen expenses.
   - Aim for three to six months' worth of living expenses in your emergency fund.

7. Monitor Debt:
   - If applicable, include debt repayment as a category in your budget.
   - Prioritize high-interest debt and consider debt reduction strategies.

8. Save for Retirement:
   - Allocate funds to retirement savings, considering employer-sponsored plans (e.g., 401(k)) and individual retirement accounts (IRAs).

9. Utilize Technology:
   - Explore budgeting apps to streamline tracking and categorizing expenses.
   - Leverage automation to facilitate regular savings and debt payments.

10. Seek Professional Guidance:
   - Consider consulting with a financial advisor for personalized advice, especially for complex financial goals such as investing or retirement planning.

In conclusion, budgeting is a dynamic and adaptable process that can be tailored to suit individual preferences and financial circumstances. The key is to choose a budgeting technique that aligns with your goals, lifestyle, and values while providing the structure needed to achieve financial success. Whether you opt for traditional methods, embrace digital solutions, or create a hybrid approach, the overarching goal is to empower yourself to make informed financial decisions, prioritize your financial well-being, and work toward achieving your unique financial aspirations.

An emergency fund is a financial safety net designed to cover unexpected expenses or income disruptions, providing individuals and families with a crucial buffer against financial stress. The essentials of an emergency fund encompass its purpose, the recommended amount, where to keep it, and strategies for building and maintaining this financial cushion.

1. Purpose of an Emergency Fund:

The primary purpose of an emergency fund is to provide financial security during unforeseen circumstances. Life is unpredictable, and unexpected events such as medical emergencies, car repairs, job loss, or home repairs can disrupt financial stability. An emergency fund serves as a protective measure, offering peace of mind and ensuring that individuals can navigate these challenges without resorting to high-interest debt or depleting long-term savings.

2. Determining the Adequate Amount:

The appropriate size of an emergency fund varies based on individual circumstances, such as income, expenses, and financial goals. However, a commonly recommended guideline is to aim for three to six months' worth of living expenses. This ensures a sufficient financial cushion to cover essential costs during a temporary loss of income or unexpected expenses.

- Living Expenses: Calculate your monthly living expenses, including housing, utilities, groceries, insurance, and debt obligations. Multiply this amount by the desired number of months (e.g., three to six) to determine your target emergency fund size.

- Consider Personal Factors: Adjust the target amount based on personal factors such as job stability, industry volatility, and individual risk tolerance. Those with irregular income or greater uncertainty may opt for a larger emergency fund.

 3. Where to Keep Your Emergency Fund:

The accessibility and safety of an emergency fund are crucial considerations. While it should be easily accessible in times of need, it should also be protected from everyday spending impulses. Here are common options:

- Savings Account: A traditional savings account at a bank or credit union is a popular choice. It offers liquidity, typically has no withdrawal restrictions, and provides a modest interest rate. Ensure the account is separate from your everyday checking account to avoid unintentional spending.

- Money Market Account: Similar to a savings account, a money market account offers liquidity and a slightly higher interest rate. Some accounts may have limited check-writing abilities, providing a bit more flexibility.

- Certificates of Deposit (CDs): While CDs offer higher interest rates, they come with a fixed term and penalties for early withdrawal. They are suitable for portions of the emergency fund that might not be needed immediately.

- High-Yield Savings Account: Online banks often offer higher interest rates than traditional banks. While these accounts may offer better returns, ensure the account is FDIC-insured and understand any associated fees or restrictions.

4. Building Your Emergency Fund:

Building an emergency fund is a gradual process that requires consistent effort and discipline. Here are effective strategies to accumulate the necessary funds:

- Set Realistic Goals: Break down your target into smaller, achievable milestones. Start with a goal for one month's worth of expenses, then gradually work towards the larger target.

- Automate Savings: Set up automatic transfers from your primary checking account to your designated emergency fund account. Treating it as a non-negotiable monthly expense ensures consistent contributions.

- Allocate Windfalls: Direct unexpected windfalls, such as tax refunds, work bonuses, or gifts, toward your emergency fund. This accelerates the accumulation process without affecting your regular budget.

- Cut Unnecessary Expenses: Review your budget and identify areas where you can reduce discretionary spending. Channel the savings directly into your emergency fund.

- Side Hustles or Gig Economy Work: Consider leveraging additional income streams, such as part-time work, freelance projects, or a side business, to boost your emergency fund.

5. When to Use Your Emergency Fund:

It's essential to distinguish between genuine emergencies and regular, planned expenses. An emergency fund should be reserved for unforeseen circumstances that could significantly impact your financial well-being. Examples include:

- Medical Emergencies: Unexpected medical expenses not covered by insurance.
- Job Loss: Loss of employment resulting in a temporary reduction or cessation of income.
- Major Car Repairs: Unanticipated repairs essential for transportation.
- Home Repairs: Urgent repairs to ensure a safe and habitable living environment.

Avoid dipping into your emergency fund for non-urgent or discretionary spending. By preserving its integrity for genuine emergencies, you maintain financial resilience.

6. Replenishing Your Emergency Fund:

Once you've used your emergency fund, focus on replenishing it as quickly as possible. Consider these strategies:

- Adjust Budget Priorities: Temporarily redirect discretionary spending towards rebuilding your emergency fund.

- Use Windfalls Wisely: Allocate unexpected windfalls, such as a tax refund or bonus, towards replenishing the fund.
- Increase Income: Explore opportunities for additional income through side gigs or part-time work.

7. Adjusting Your Emergency Fund Over Time:

As your life circumstances change, periodically reassess and adjust your emergency fund. Consider the following factors:

- Changes in Income: If your income significantly increases or decreases, adjust your emergency fund target accordingly.
- Life Events: Marriage, having children, or other significant life events may necessitate a reassessment of your emergency fund needs.
- Cost of Living Changes: If you relocate to an area with a higher or lower cost of living, adjust your emergency fund to reflect these changes.

8. Maintain Flexibility:

While the three to six months' guideline is commonly recommended, personal circumstances may warrant a different approach. Individuals with stable employment, dual-income households, or significant liquid assets may feel comfortable with a smaller emergency fund. Conversely, those with irregular income or a higher level of financial uncertainty may opt for a more substantial buffer.

In summary, an emergency fund is a foundational element of financial well-being, providing a sense of security and resilience in the face of unexpected challenges. Determining the appropriate size, choosing suitable storage options, and employing effective strategies for building and replenishing the fund are essential components of financial planning. By understanding the purpose and essentials of an emergency fund, individuals can navigate life's uncertainties with greater confidence, knowing they have a financial safety net in place.

CHAPTER 3: Investing in Knowledge

Financial literacy is a critical life skill that empowers individuals to make informed and effective decisions regarding their money. It involves understanding various aspects of personal finance, including budgeting, saving, investing, debt management, and overall financial planning. The importance of financial literacy extends far beyond the realm of individual well-being; it influences economic stability, societal progress, and the ability of individuals to achieve their financial goals.

1. Empowerment and Control:

Financial literacy empowers individuals to take control of their financial destinies. When people understand how to manage their money effectively, they gain a sense of control over their financial situation. This control extends to budgeting, saving, investing, and making informed decisions about credit and debt. Financially literate individuals are more likely to navigate financial challenges with confidence, reducing stress and fostering a sense of empowerment.

2. Improved Financial Decision-Making:

Financial literacy enhances decision-making skills, enabling individuals to make choices that align with their goals and values. From choosing appropriate investment options to understanding the implications of taking on debt, financially literate individuals can assess the potential outcomes of their decisions. This leads to more prudent financial choices, reducing the likelihood of financial pitfalls and regrets.

3. Budgeting and Expense Management:

One of the fundamental aspects of financial literacy is the ability to create and maintain a budget. Budgeting involves allocating income to various expenses, savings, and investments. Financially literate individuals can develop realistic budgets that prioritize essential expenses while allowing for savings and discretionary spending. This skill is crucial for living within one's means, avoiding debt, and building a solid financial foundation.

4. Savings and Emergency Preparedness:

Financial literacy emphasizes the importance of saving for both short-term and long-term goals. Understanding the value of saving enables individuals to build emergency funds, providing a financial cushion for unexpected expenses or income disruptions. A well-funded emergency fund is a key component of financial resilience, reducing reliance on credit during challenging times.

5. Investing for the Future:

Investing is a powerful wealth-building tool, and financial literacy is essential for understanding the various investment options and strategies. Financially literate individuals can make informed decisions about investing in stocks, bonds, mutual funds, real estate, and other vehicles. This knowledge empowers them to grow their wealth over time and work towards achieving long-term financial goals such as retirement.

6. Debt Management:

Understanding the implications of debt and how to manage it effectively is a critical aspect of financial literacy. Financially literate individuals can evaluate different types of debt, distinguish between good and bad debt, and develop strategies for debt repayment. This knowledge helps in avoiding excessive debt, minimizing interest costs, and maintaining a healthy credit profile.

7. Financial Goal Setting:

Financial literacy encourages individuals to set clear and achievable financial goals. Whether it's buying a home, starting a business, or saving for education, setting specific, measurable, and time-bound goals provides a roadmap for financial success. Financially literate individuals can break down larger goals into manageable steps, increasing the likelihood of successful goal attainment.

8. Protection Against Financial Fraud:

Financial literacy includes awareness of common financial scams and fraud. Being able to recognize red flags and understanding how to protect personal and financial information is crucial in an increasingly digital and interconnected world. Financially literate individuals are less likely to fall victim to scams and identity theft.

9. Generational Wealth and Legacy Planning:

Financial literacy extends to understanding the concept of generational wealth and legacy planning. It involves making strategic financial decisions that not only benefit the present generation but also contribute to the financial well-being of future generations. This may include estate planning, creating trusts, and passing on financial knowledge and values to heirs.

10. Economic Stability and Societal Progress:

On a broader scale, the importance of financial literacy is evident in its impact on economic stability and societal progress. A financially literate population contributes to a more stable economy. Individuals who are adept at managing their finances are less likely to rely on social safety nets, reducing the overall burden on public resources. This, in turn, contributes to societal progress by fostering economic resilience and independence.

11. Workplace Productivity and Well-Being:

Financial stress can significantly impact an individual's well-being and workplace productivity. Financially literate individuals are better equipped to manage their finances, reducing stress and distractions related to money concerns. This, in turn, enhances workplace productivity and contributes to a healthier work environment.

12. Entrepreneurship and Innovation:

Financial literacy is a key factor in fostering entrepreneurship and innovation. Individuals with a solid understanding of financial principles are more likely to take calculated risks, start businesses, and contribute to economic growth. Entrepreneurial endeavors often require financial acumen to secure funding, manage cash flow, and navigate the complexities of business finance.

13. Inclusivity and Social Justice:

Promoting financial literacy is crucial for creating a more inclusive society. Access to financial education and resources should be equitable, ensuring that individuals from diverse socioeconomic backgrounds have the knowledge and tools to make informed financial decisions. Financial literacy contributes to social justice by reducing disparities in financial outcomes.

14. Adaptability in Changing Economic Conditions:

In a dynamic economic landscape, individuals with financial literacy are better equipped to adapt to changing conditions. Whether it's navigating economic downturns, adjusting investment strategies, or exploring new career opportunities, financial literacy provides the agility to make informed decisions in response to evolving circumstances.

15. Global Economic Competence:

As the world becomes more interconnected, understanding global economic forces and trends is increasingly important

Financial literacy extends beyond personal finance to encompass an understanding of global economic factors. In a globalized economy, events in one part of the world can have ripple effects across borders. Financially literate individuals are better positioned to comprehend these interconnected dynamics, make informed decisions about international investments, and navigate the complexities of a global marketplace.

In conclusion, the importance of financial literacy cannot be overstated in the context of individual well-being, economic stability, and societal progress. Financially literate individuals are empowered to make informed decisions about their money, from day-to-day budgeting to long-term investment strategies. This empowerment extends to their ability to weather financial challenges, pursue their goals, and contribute to the overall prosperity of society.

Efforts to promote financial literacy should be comprehensive and inclusive, targeting individuals at various stages of life and socioeconomic backgrounds. Educational initiatives, both formal and informal, play a crucial role in equipping people with the knowledge and skills needed to navigate the complex world of personal finance. Governments, educational institutions, employers, and community organizations all have a role to play in fostering financial literacy.

As we recognize the multifaceted benefits of financial literacy, it becomes clear that it is not merely a personal asset but a societal imperative. A financially literate population contributes to economic resilience, reduces the burden on public resources, and fosters a culture of informed decision-making. In an era of constant economic change and financial complexity, the value of financial literacy extends far beyond individual bank accounts—it is an investment in the collective well-being and progress of society as a whole.

Educational resources and tools are essential components of effective learning in today's digital age. As technology continues to advance, the educational landscape has been transformed, providing learners with a wealth of resources and tools to enhance their knowledge and skills. From online courses and interactive platforms to specialized software and collaborative tools, the availability of educational resources has expanded, making learning more accessible and engaging. In this exploration, we will delve into various educational resources and tools, highlighting their significance in fostering effective learning.

1. Online Courses and MOOCs:

Online courses and Massive Open Online Courses (MOOCs) have revolutionized the way people access education. Platforms like Coursera, edX, and Udacity offer a vast array of courses covering diverse subjects, from computer science and business to humanities and the sciences. Learners can enroll in courses offered by renowned universities and institutions worldwide, providing an opportunity for flexible, self-paced learning. These platforms often include video lectures, interactive quizzes, and discussion forums, creating a dynamic and engaging learning environment.

2. E-Learning Platforms:

E-learning platforms, such as Khan Academy and Skillshare, provide a variety of educational content, including video lessons, interactive exercises, and project-based learning. Khan Academy, for instance, offers free educational resources in subjects like mathematics, science, and humanities, catering to learners of all ages. Skillshare focuses on creative skills, offering classes in art, design, writing, and more. These platforms democratize access to education, allowing individuals to learn at their own pace and explore areas of interest beyond traditional academic subjects.

3. Interactive Learning Apps:

Educational apps have become powerful tools for interactive and personalized learning. Apps like Duolingo for language learning, Quizlet for flashcards and quizzes, and Photomath for mathematics problem-solving offer engaging and accessible ways to reinforce concepts. These apps often incorporate gamified elements, making learning enjoyable and motivating learners to progress through challenges and achievements.

4. Digital Libraries and Open Educational Resources (OER):

Digital libraries and OER platforms provide free access to a wealth of educational materials. Websites like Project Gutenberg offer a vast collection of classic literature, while platforms like OpenStax provide free, peer-reviewed textbooks for college courses. These resources eliminate financial barriers to education, making quality content available to learners worldwide. Libraries and institutions also increasingly offer digital access to books, articles, and research materials, expanding the reach of information.

5. Educational Software and Simulations:

Educational software and simulations enhance learning by providing interactive and immersive experiences. For example, software like GeoGebra supports mathematics learning through dynamic visualizations, while virtual dissection tools offer a realistic exploration of biology without the need for physical specimens. Simulations in science, engineering, and other fields allow learners to experiment and observe outcomes, fostering a deeper understanding of complex concepts.

6. Learning Management Systems (LMS):

Learning Management Systems, such as Moodle and Canvas, are platforms that facilitate the administration, documentation, tracking, and delivery of educational courses. These systems are widely used in academic institutions and organizations for creating and managing online courses. LMSs provide tools for content delivery, assessments, and collaboration, streamlining the learning experience for both educators and learners.

7. Collaboration Tools and Virtual Classrooms:

Collaboration tools and virtual classrooms have become indispensable for remote and blended learning environments. Platforms like Zoom, Microsoft Teams, and Google Meet enable real-time communication, video conferencing, and collaboration among learners and educators. Virtual classrooms integrate features like breakout rooms, screen sharing, and collaborative documents, fostering interactive and engaging learning experiences.

8. Coding Platforms and STEM Tools:

With the increasing emphasis on STEM (Science, Technology, Engineering, and Mathematics) education, coding platforms and STEM tools play a crucial role in developing computational thinking and problem-solving skills. Platforms like Scratch and Code.org introduce coding concepts through visual programming, making it accessible to learners of all ages. Hardware kits and platforms, such as Raspberry Pi and Arduino, allow hands-on exploration of electronics and programming.

9. Educational Podcasts and Audiobooks:

Podcasts and audiobooks provide a convenient way to consume educational content while on the go. Platforms like TED Talks, NPR Education, and educational podcasts covering a wide range of subjects offer in-depth discussions, interviews, and insights. Audiobooks, available through platforms like Audible, provide an alternative means of accessing literature and educational material, catering to different learning preferences.

10. Language Learning Platforms:

Language learning platforms, such as Rosetta Stone, Babbel, and Memrise, leverage technology to teach languages through interactive exercises, immersive experiences, and gamified approaches. These platforms often incorporate speech recognition technology to enhance language pronunciation and fluency. Learners can practice languages at their own pace and receive instant feedback, facilitating effective language acquisition.

11. Adaptive Learning Systems:

Adaptive learning systems utilize technology to personalize the learning experience based on individual progress and performance. These systems, like Smart Sparrow and Knewton, adjust content and assessments in real-time, tailoring the learning path to each learner's strengths and weaknesses. Adaptive learning promotes efficiency by focusing on areas that need improvement, allowing learners to advance at their own optimal pace.

12. Augmented Reality (AR) and Virtual Reality (VR):

AR and VR technologies offer immersive learning experiences that go beyond traditional methods. AR enhances the real-world environment with digital overlays, providing interactive and contextual information. VR, on the other hand, creates simulated environments, allowing learners to explore and interact with three-dimensional content. These technologies find applications in fields such as anatomy, history, and vocational training, providing realistic and engaging learning scenarios.

13. Financial Literacy Platforms:

Given the importance of financial literacy, specialized platforms like Mint, Personal Capital, and educational modules within banking apps provide tools to enhance financial knowledge. These platforms help users manage budgets, track spending, and gain insights into their financial habits. Educational modules often cover topics like savings, investments, and debt management, contributing to increased financial literacy.

14. Digital Citizenship Education:

With the rise of digital interactions, digital citizenship education has become crucial. Platforms like Common Sense Education offer resources and tools to teach students about responsible and ethical use of technology, online safety, and digital communication. Digital citizenship education equips learners with the skills to navigate the digital world responsibly and ethically.

15. Accessibility and Inclusivity Tools:

Educational resources and tools should be designed with inclusivity in mind. Accessibility tools, such as screen readers, closed captions, and alternative text descriptions, ensure that content is accessible to individuals with disabilities. Inclusive design principles, such as Universal Design for Learning (UDL), aim to create educational materials that accommodate diverse learning styles and abilities.

Conclusion:

Educational resources and tools have transformed the learning landscape, providing individuals with unprecedented access to knowledge and skills. From traditional subjects to emerging technologies, these resources cater to diverse learning styles and preferences. As technology continues to advance, the ongoing development and integration of innovative educational tools will play a pivotal role in shaping the future of learning. Embracing these resources empowers learners to explore, collaborate, and engage in lifelong learning journeys, fostering a society that values education as a cornerstone of personal and societal progress.

CHAPTER 4: Earning Beyond a Paycheck

Exploring additional income streams is a strategic approach to enhance financial stability, achieve specific financial goals, or create a buffer against economic uncertainties. Diversifying income sources can provide both short-term financial gains and long-term financial security. Here are various avenues to explore when seeking additional income streams:

1. Freelancing and Consulting:

Utilize your skills and expertise to offer freelance services or consulting in your field. Websites like Upwork, Freelancer, and Fiverr connect freelancers with clients seeking specific services, ranging from writing and graphic design to programming and marketing. Consulting opportunities may involve providing specialized advice to businesses or individuals based on your professional experience.

2. Online Courses and Ebooks:

If you possess expertise in a particular subject, consider creating and selling online courses or ebooks. Platforms like Udemy, Teachable, and Amazon Kindle Direct Publishing allow you to reach a global audience. Share your knowledge on topics such as programming, photography, business strategies, or any area where you have expertise.

3. Investing:

Investing can be a passive income stream if done wisely. Explore various investment options, including stocks, bonds, real estate, or mutual funds. Dividend-paying stocks can provide regular income, and real estate investments may generate rental income. Keep in mind that investing involves risks, and it's essential to conduct thorough research or consult with a financial advisor before making investment decisions.

4. Peer-to-Peer Lending:

Participate in peer-to-peer lending platforms that connect borrowers with individual lenders. Websites like Prosper or LendingClub allow you to lend money to individuals or small businesses in exchange for interest payments. While there are risks associated with lending, it can be a way to earn passive income through interest.

5. Rental Income:

If you have extra space, consider renting it out for additional income. This could include renting a room on platforms like Airbnb or leasing a property you own. Renting out assets, such as equipment or tools, is also an option for those with specific items in demand.

6. Side Hustles and Gig Economy Work:

Engage in side hustles or gig economy work to supplement your income. This could involve driving for ride-sharing services, delivering groceries or food, or offering services on platforms like TaskRabbit. Many people find success by combining multiple gig economy opportunities.

7. Affiliate Marketing:

Explore affiliate marketing by promoting products or services and earning a commission for each sale made through your referral. Join affiliate programs related to your niche or interests, and use platforms like Amazon Associates or affiliate networks to find products you can endorse. Bloggers, YouTubers, and social media influencers often leverage affiliate marketing.

8. Create and Sell Crafts:

If you're skilled in crafting, consider creating and selling handmade products. Platforms like Etsy provide a marketplace for artisans to sell unique and personalized items. Whether it's jewelry, artwork, or customized home decor, there's a market for handmade goods.

9. Participate in Market Research:

Sign up for market research panels or online surveys to provide feedback on products and services. Companies often pay for consumer opinions, and participating in surveys or focus groups can be a flexible way to earn extra income. Websites like

Survey Junkie or Swagbucks offer opportunities to earn rewards for participating in surveys.

10. Real Estate Crowdfunding:

Investing in real estate through crowdfunding platforms allows you to pool funds with other investors to collectively invest in real estate projects. This can provide exposure to real estate without the need for large capital. Platforms like Fundrise or RealtyMogul offer opportunities for real estate crowdfunding.

11. Create a YouTube Channel:

If you enjoy creating content, consider starting a YouTube channel. Monetize your videos through ads, sponsorships, or memberships. Successful YouTubers cover a wide range of topics, from educational content and product reviews to entertainment and lifestyle vlogs.

12. Remote Work Opportunities:

Explore remote work opportunities in your field or in areas where you have relevant skills. Many companies offer remote work options, and various job boards focus specifically on remote positions. Websites like Remote OK and FlexJobs can help you find remote work opportunities.

13. Photography and Stock Images:

If you have photography skills, consider selling your photos to stock image websites. Platforms like Shutterstock, Adobe Stock, or iStock allow photographers to upload and sell their images, providing a potential source of passive income.

14. Podcasting:

Create a podcast around a topic you are passionate about. Monetization options include sponsorships, listener donations, or premium content for subscribers. As your podcast grows in popularity, it has the potential to generate income over time.

15. Offer Online Tutoring or Coaching:

If you excel in a particular subject or have expertise in a specific area, offer online tutoring or coaching services. Platforms like Chegg Tutors, Wyzant, or

Teachable allow you to connect with learners seeking guidance and support.

 Final Thoughts:

Exploring additional income streams requires a combination of creativity, initiative, and leveraging your existing skills and interests. Diversifying your income sources not only provides financial resilience but also opens up opportunities for personal and professional growth. It's essential to assess your strengths, interests, and available resources when choosing the potential source for additional income.

Developing an entrepreneurial mindset is a transformative journey that goes beyond starting a business; it involves cultivating a unique way of thinking and approaching challenges. An entrepreneurial mindset encompasses a set of attitudes, skills, and behaviors that empower individuals to identify opportunities, take calculated risks, and persist in the face of adversity. Whether you aspire to launch a startup, excel in your career, or simply approach life with a problem-solving mindset, developing an entrepreneurial mindset is a valuable pursuit.

1. Vision and Opportunity Recognition:

An entrepreneurial mindset begins with the ability to see beyond the status quo. Entrepreneurs possess a vision—a clear picture of the future they want to create. This visionary thinking allows individuals to identify opportunities where others see challenges. Whether in business, technology, or personal endeavors, the capacity to recognize opportunities is the cornerstone of entrepreneurial success.

2. Risk-Taking and Tolerance for Uncertainty:

Entrepreneurship inherently involves risk, and cultivating an entrepreneurial mindset means developing a comfort with uncertainty. Entrepreneurs understand that calculated risks are often necessary for innovation and growth. They embrace challenges as learning opportunities, recognizing that failure is not a setback but a stepping stone toward success.

3. Adaptability and Flexibility:

The entrepreneurial journey is dynamic, marked by constant change and unexpected turns. Those with an entrepreneurial mindset embrace change and adapt quickly to evolving circumstances. This adaptability is essential not only in the face of challenges but also for seizing new opportunities that may arise unexpectedly.

4. Initiative and Proactivity:

Entrepreneurs are known for taking initiative and being proactive in pursuing their goals. An entrepreneurial mindset involves a bias toward action—being proactive rather than reactive. This mindset encourages individuals to seek out opportunities, create solutions, and take the lead in shaping their own paths.

5. Continuous Learning and Curiosity:

A commitment to continuous learning is a hallmark of the entrepreneurial mindset. Entrepreneurs are naturally curious, driven to explore new ideas, industries, and technologies. They see every experience as a chance to acquire knowledge and enhance their skill set, fostering a growth-oriented mindset that propels them forward.

6. Resilience and Perseverance:

Resilience is a critical component of the entrepreneurial mindset. The ability to bounce back from setbacks, adapt to challenges, and persevere in the face of adversity is what sets entrepreneurs apart. Developing resilience involves cultivating a positive mindset, maintaining focus on long-term goals, and viewing failures as valuable lessons.

7. Customer-Centric Thinking:

Entrepreneurs prioritize understanding the needs and preferences of their target audience. This customer-centric thinking is not limited to business ventures—it extends to any context where solutions are designed to address the needs of others. An entrepreneurial mindset involves empathy and a genuine desire to create value for others.

8. Networking and Relationship Building:

Building and nurturing relationships is a key aspect of entrepreneurship. An entrepreneurial mindset involves recognizing the value of networks—whether for mentorship, collaboration, or accessing resources. Successful entrepreneurs understand the power of connecting with others and leveraging these relationships for mutual benefit.

9. Resource Optimization:

Entrepreneurs are adept at making the most of available resources. An entrepreneurial mindset involves resource optimization—whether it's time, money, or talent. This skill requires creative problem-solving and the ability to leverage existing assets efficiently, fostering a mindset of resourcefulness.

10. Results-Driven Orientation:

An entrepreneurial mindset is results-oriented. Entrepreneurs set clear goals and are focused on achieving measurable outcomes. This orientation toward results instills a sense of accountability and drive, pushing individuals to take purposeful actions that contribute to their objectives.

11. Innovative Thinking and Creativity:

Innovation is at the heart of entrepreneurship. An entrepreneurial mindset involves thinking creatively and seeking innovative solutions to problems. This involves challenging the status quo, thinking outside the box, and being open to unconventional approaches.

12. Financial Literacy:

Understanding basic financial principles is crucial for entrepreneurial success. An entrepreneurial mindset includes financial literacy—knowing how to manage finances, make informed financial decisions, and assess the financial viability of ideas or ventures.

13. Leadership and Team Collaboration:

Entrepreneurs often find themselves in leadership roles, whether leading a startup or influencing change within an organization. An entrepreneurial mindset involves developing leadership skills, including effective communication, decision-making, and the ability to inspire and motivate others. Additionally, collaboration with diverse teams is recognized as essential for innovation and success.

14. Ethical Decision-Making:

Ethical considerations are integral to the entrepreneurial mindset. Entrepreneurs prioritize ethical decision-making and integrity in their actions. This commitment to ethical standards builds trust with stakeholders and contributes to long-term success.

15. Global Perspective:

In an increasingly interconnected world, entrepreneurs with a global perspective are better equipped to navigate diverse markets and cultural landscapes. An entrepreneurial mindset involves understanding global trends, recognizing international opportunities, and appreciating cultural nuances. This global awareness allows entrepreneurs to identify untapped markets, forge international partnerships, and adapt their strategies to a rapidly evolving global economy.

16. Environmental and Social Responsibility:

Entrepreneurs with an entrepreneurial mindset recognize the importance of environmental and social responsibility. They understand that businesses and individuals can contribute positively to society and the environment. This mindset involves considering the impact of decisions on the community, environment, and future generations, promoting sustainability and responsible business practices.

17. Learning from Feedback:

An entrepreneurial mindset involves being open to feedback and viewing it as a valuable tool for growth. Whether from customers, peers, or mentors, feedback provides insights that can inform improvements and innovations. Embracing constructive criticism and using it to refine ideas or approaches is a hallmark of an entrepreneurial mindset.

18. Data-Driven Decision-Making:

Entrepreneurs rely on data to make informed decisions. An entrepreneurial mindset involves the ability to gather, analyze, and interpret data to guide strategic choices. This data-driven approach ensures that decisions are based on evidence and align with overarching goals.

19. Embracing Technology and Digital Transformation:

In the digital age, an entrepreneurial mindset includes a willingness to embrace technology and navigate digital transformations. Entrepreneurs leverage technology to streamline processes, reach wider audiences, and stay ahead of industry trends. This adaptability to technological advancements is vital for remaining competitive and relevant.

20. Experimentation and Iteration:

Entrepreneurs are not afraid to experiment and iterate on their ideas. The entrepreneurial mindset involves a willingness to test hypotheses, learn from outcomes, and refine approaches. This iterative process allows for continuous improvement and innovation.

21. Goal Setting and Strategic Planning:

Entrepreneurs are skilled at setting clear goals and developing strategic plans to achieve them. An entrepreneurial mindset involves breaking down larger objectives into actionable steps and milestones. This goal-oriented thinking provides a roadmap for progress and success.

22. Passion and Purpose:

Passion and a sense of purpose are driving forces behind the entrepreneurial mindset. Entrepreneurs are often deeply passionate about their ventures, which fuels their determination and resilience. This passion is infectious, motivating others and creating a sense of purpose that goes beyond financial success.

23. Mindfulness and Mental Resilience:

Cultivating an entrepreneurial mindset involves mindfulness and mental resilience. The ability to stay focused, manage stress, and maintain a positive outlook amid challenges is crucial. Mindfulness practices, such as meditation or stress-reducing activities, contribute to mental resilience, enhancing an individual's ability to navigate the entrepreneurial journey.

24. Networking and Community Engagement:

Entrepreneurs recognize the value of networking and actively engage with their communities. Building a supportive network of peers, mentors, and industry connections provides valuable insights, opportunities, and a sense of community. Networking is not only about personal advancement but also about contributing to the growth and success of others.

25. Celebration of Success and Learning from Failure:

An entrepreneurial mindset involves celebrating successes, no matter how small, and acknowledging achievements along the way. Additionally, entrepreneurs view failures as learning experiences rather than insurmountable obstacles. This resilience in the face of setbacks contributes to personal and professional growth.

In essence, developing an entrepreneurial mindset is a holistic and ongoing process that transcends the traditional boundaries of business. It is a mindset that can be applied to various aspects of life, from personal development and career advancement to societal contributions and innovation. Entrepreneurs continually refine and expand their mindset as they encounter new challenges and opportunities.

The entrepreneurial mindset is not exclusive to those launching startups; it's a mindset that empowers individuals to approach life with creativity, resilience, and a proactive attitude. By embracing the key attributes discussed—vision, risk-taking, adaptability, continuous learning, and more—individuals can unlock their entrepreneurial potential, fostering a mindset that thrives in a dynamic and ever-changing world. Ultimately, the entrepreneurial mindset is a catalyst for personal and collective progress, driving innovation, positive change, and the pursuit of meaningful goals.

CHAPTER 5: Managing Debts Strategically

Debt is a financial obligation that arises when one party borrows money from another with the promise of repaying the borrowed amount along with interest. Understanding the different types of debts is crucial for making informed financial decisions and managing one's financial well-being. Debts can be broadly categorized into various types, each with its own characteristics, terms, and implications.

1. Secured Debt:

Secured debt is backed by collateral, which is an asset that serves as security for the loan. If the borrower fails to repay the debt, the lender can seize the collateral to recover the amount owed. Common examples of secured debts include:

- Mortgages: Home loans are secured by the property being purchased.
- Auto Loans: Vehicle loans are secured by the financed vehicle.

- Secured Personal Loans: Some personal loans are secured by assets such as savings accounts or certificates of deposit.

Secured debts typically have lower interest rates compared to unsecured debts because the collateral mitigates the lender's risk.

 2. Unsecured Debt:

Unsecured debt does not require collateral, relying solely on the borrower's creditworthiness and promise to repay. Because these debts pose a higher risk to lenders, interest rates are generally higher. Common types of unsecured debts include:

- Credit Cards: Revolving credit lines that don't require collateral.
- Personal Loans: Unsecured loans for various purposes, such as debt consolidation or home improvements.
- Student Loans: Loans for education expenses that may or may not be backed by government guarantees.

Due to the absence of collateral, lenders rely heavily on the borrower's credit history and income when approving unsecured debt.

3. Revolving Debt:

Revolving debt allows borrowers to repeatedly borrow up to a certain credit limit, repay, and borrow again. The outstanding balance fluctuates based on usage and payments. Credit cards are a common form of revolving debt. The key features of revolving debt include:

- Flexibility: Borrowers can use available credit up to their limit.
- Variable Interest Rates: Interest rates can change based on market conditions or creditworthiness.
- Minimum Payments: Borrowers must make at least the minimum monthly payment.

Effectively managing revolving debt involves understanding interest rates, payment terms, and avoiding excessive balances.

4. Installment Debt:

Installment debt involves borrowing a specific amount and repaying it in fixed, regular installments over a predetermined period. The structure of installment debt is predictable, making it easier for borrowers to budget. Common examples include:

- Auto Loans: Monthly payments over a set term to finance a vehicle.
- Personal Loans: Fixed-term loans for various purposes.
- Mortgages: Home loans with regular payments over the loan term.

Installment debt often has a fixed interest rate, simplifying budgeting and long-term financial planning.

5. Open-End Credit:

Open-end credit provides a revolving line of credit with no fixed end date. Borrowers can borrow, repay, and borrow again. Credit cards and lines of credit are examples of open-end credit. Key characteristics include:

- Flexible Spending: Borrowers can use the credit line as needed.
- Variable Interest Rates: Interest rates may change based on market conditions.
- Minimum Payments: Borrowers are required to make minimum monthly payments.

Open-end credit offers convenience but requires disciplined management to avoid accumulating high balances.

6. Closed-End Credit:

Closed-end credit provides a one-time loan for a specific purpose with a fixed repayment term. Once the borrower repays the loan, the credit line is closed. Mortgages and auto loans are common examples of closed-end credit. Features include:

- Fixed Loan Amount: Borrowers receive a specific amount.
- Fixed Interest Rates: Interest rates remain constant throughout the loan term.
- Structured Repayment: Monthly payments follow a set schedule.

Closed-end credit is suitable for specific needs, such as purchasing a home or financing a major expense.

7. Corporate Debt:

Corporate debt refers to money borrowed by businesses to fund operations, expansion, or other financial needs. Companies may issue bonds or take loans to raise capital. Key aspects of corporate debt include:

- Bond Issuance: Companies may issue bonds that investors purchase, providing capital to the company.
- Bank Loans: Businesses secure loans from financial institutions to finance projects or operations.
- Debentures: Unsecured corporate bonds backed only by the company's creditworthiness.

Understanding corporate debt is essential for investors assessing the financial health of companies and their investment portfolios.

8. Government Debt:

Governments may incur debt to fund public projects, infrastructure, or manage budget deficits. Government debt can be categorized into:

- Treasury Bonds: Long-term debt securities issued by governments.
- Treasury Bills: Short-term debt securities with maturities typically less than one year.
- Government Loans: Borrowings from international organizations or other governments.

Government debt plays a crucial role in economic management but requires careful monitoring to maintain fiscal health.

9. Consumer Debt:

Consumer debt is debt incurred by individuals for personal consumption rather than investment. This includes various forms of borrowing to finance daily expenses, purchases, or emergencies. Common types of consumer debt include:

- Credit Card Balances: Outstanding balances on credit cards.
- Personal Loans: Borrowings for personal expenses.

- Payday Loans: Short-term loans with high interest rates.

Managing consumer debt is vital for individuals to maintain financial health and avoid excessive interest payments.

10. Medical Debt:

Medical debt arises when individuals cannot afford healthcare expenses and must borrow to cover medical bills. This type of debt can result from unexpected medical emergencies, treatments, or procedures. Key considerations include:

- Payment Plans: Hospitals may offer payment plans to help individuals manage medical debt.
- Negotiation: Individuals can negotiate with healthcare providers to reduce or settle medical bills.
- Financial Assistance Programs: Some hospitals offer financial assistance or charity care.

Addressing medical debt often involves communication with healthcare providers and exploring available assistance options.

Understanding the different types of debts is essential for making informed financial decisions and managing debt responsibly. Each type of debt comes with its own terms, risks, and potential impact on personal or business finances. By recognizing the characteristics of various debts, individuals and businesses can develop effective strategies for borrowing, repayment, and overall financial well-being. Careful consideration of the purpose, terms, and implications of debt is crucial to maintaining a healthy financial balance and achieving long-term financial goals.

Debt reduction is a crucial aspect of achieving financial stability and building a secure financial future. Whether dealing with credit card debt, student loans, or other financial obligations, adopting effective debt reduction strategies can make a significant difference. Here are key debt reduction strategies to help individuals regain control of their finances and work towards a debt-free life:

1. Create a Detailed Budget:

The foundation of effective debt reduction is a well-structured budget. Start by listing all sources of income and categorizing monthly expenses. Differentiate between essential expenses (such as housing, utilities, and groceries) and discretionary spending (such as entertainment and dining out). A clear budget provides a snapshot of financial inflows and outflows, enabling informed decision-making.

2. Identify and Prioritize Debts:

Compile a list of all outstanding debts, including balances, interest rates, and minimum monthly payments. Prioritize debts based on interest rates, with higher interest debts taking precedence. While continuing to make minimum payments on all debts, allocate any extra funds towards the highest interest debt. This strategy minimizes the overall interest paid and accelerates the debt reduction process.

3. Implement the Debt Snowball Method:

Popularized by personal finance expert Dave Ramsey, the debt snowball method focuses on paying off the smallest debts first. Start by tackling the smallest debt while maintaining minimum payments on others. Once the smallest debt is paid off, redirect the funds towards the next smallest debt. This method provides psychological wins, as individuals experience a sense of accomplishment with each debt paid off, motivating them to continue the debt reduction journey.

4. Negotiate Lower Interest Rates:

Contact creditors and negotiate lower interest rates, especially if you have a good payment history. Lower interest rates mean more of your payment goes towards reducing the principal amount, accelerating the debt payoff process. Be prepared to present your case, emphasizing your commitment to repaying the debt and highlighting any improvements in your financial situation.

5. Debt Consolidation:

Consolidating multiple debts into a single, lower-interest loan can simplify repayment and reduce overall interest costs. Options for debt consolidation include balance transfer credit cards, personal loans, or home equity loans. It's essential to carefully assess the terms, fees, and interest rates associated with consolidation options to ensure they align with your financial goals.

6. Increase Income:

Augmenting your income can provide additional funds to expedite debt repayment. Explore opportunities for a side hustle, freelancing, or a part-time job. Income from these endeavors can be dedicated entirely to debt reduction, helping you make more significant strides in paying off outstanding balances.

7. Cut Unnecessary Expenses:

Examine your discretionary spending and identify areas where you can cut back. This may involve reducing dining out, entertainment expenses, or subscription services. The money saved can be redirected towards debt repayment, accelerating the payoff process.

8. Emergency Fund:

While it may seem counterintuitive to focus on saving while in debt, having an emergency fund is crucial. Without an emergency fund, unexpected expenses can lead to accumulating more debt. Aim to build a small emergency fund—ideally, three to six months' worth of living expenses—before aggressively tackling debt. This fund acts as a financial safety net, preventing the need to rely on credit for unforeseen circumstances.

9. Use Windfalls Wisely:

Any unexpected windfalls, such as tax refunds, work bonuses, or gifts, can significantly impact your debt reduction efforts. While it might be tempting to use these funds for discretionary spending, channeling windfalls towards debt repayment provides a substantial boost to your financial goals.

10. Seek Professional Advice:

If managing debt becomes overwhelming, consider seeking advice from a financial counselor or debt management professional. They can provide personalized guidance, help negotiate with creditors, and assist in developing a tailored debt repayment plan. Be cautious when choosing debt consolidation services and ensure they are reputable and transparent about their fees.

11. Stay Committed and Stay Positive:

Debt reduction is a journey that requires commitment and perseverance. Celebrate small victories along the way, such as paying off individual debts or reaching specific milestones. Cultivate a positive mindset, focusing on the progress made rather than the remaining debt. Staying committed to the debt reduction plan, even during challenging times, is key to long-term success.

12. Consider Debt Settlement or Negotiation:

In cases of extreme financial hardship, debt settlement or negotiation may be an option. Contact creditors to discuss your situation and explore the possibility of settling the debt for a reduced amount or negotiating more favorable terms. Keep in mind that debt settlement can impact your credit score, and professional advice is recommended before pursuing this option.

13. Explore Government Assistance Programs:

Depending on the type of debt, there may be government assistance programs or repayment plans available. For example, student loans may qualify for income-driven repayment plans or loan forgiveness programs. Research available options and determine eligibility for government assistance to ease the burden of specific debts.

14. Monitor and Adjust:

Regularly review your budget, debt repayment plan, and overall financial situation. Life circumstances, income, and expenses may change, requiring adjustments to your debt reduction strategy. Be flexible and proactive in adapting your approach to align with your current financial reality.

15. Financial Education:

Invest time in educating yourself about personal finance and debt management. Understanding financial principles, interest rates, and the impact of debt on your overall financial health empowers you to make informed decisions. There are numerous online resources, books, and courses that can enhance your financial literacy.

Effective debt reduction requires a comprehensive and disciplined approach. Combining budgeting, prioritization, negotiation, and proactive financial management can pave the way to financial freedom. Each individual's financial situation is unique, so it's essential to tailor these strategies to fit your specific circumstances. By committing to a debt reduction plan and staying focused on long-term financial goals, individuals can overcome debt challenges and build a more secure financial future.

CHAPTER 6: The Power of Saving

Cultivating a savings mindset is a transformative journey that goes beyond simply stashing away money. It involves a shift in attitude and habits toward a more intentional and proactive approach to financial well-being. A savings mindset is not only about building a financial cushion but also about fostering a mindset that values long-term financial security, responsible spending, and the ability to achieve future goals. Here are key strategies to cultivate a savings mindset:

1. Set Clear Financial Goals:

Begin by defining your financial goals, both short-term and long-term. Whether it's creating an emergency fund, saving for a vacation, or planning for retirement, clear goals provide direction and motivation. Break down larger goals into smaller, achievable milestones. This clarity helps you prioritize and allocate funds purposefully.

2. Build an Emergency Fund:

An emergency fund serves as a financial safety net, providing a buffer for unexpected expenses or emergencies. Aim to save three to six months' worth of living expenses. Start small if needed, but consistently contribute to your emergency fund. Knowing you have a financial cushion can alleviate stress and prevent the need to rely on credit in times of crisis.

3. Automate Savings:

Automating your savings is a powerful strategy. Set up automatic transfers from your checking account to a savings account. Treating savings as a non-negotiable expense reinforces the habit and ensures consistent contributions. Many employers also offer automated payroll deductions for savings accounts or retirement plans.

4. Create a Realistic Budget:

Developing a realistic budget is fundamental to a savings mindset. Track your income and expenses to understand your financial landscape. Categorize spending into essentials and non-essentials. Identify areas where you can cut back and allocate those funds toward savings. A budget provides a clear overview of your financial habits and opportunities for improvement.

5. Practice Mindful Spending:

Mindful spending involves intentional and conscious decisions about where your money goes. Before making a purchase, ask yourself if it aligns with your financial goals. Differentiate between needs and wants, and prioritize spending on items that bring lasting value. This mindfulness reduces impulse purchases and redirects funds toward savings.

6. Live Below Your Means:

Cultivating a savings mindset often involves living below your means. Avoid the trap of lifestyle inflation—increasing expenses as income rises. Instead, consistently save a portion of any income increase. This approach creates a financial buffer and accelerates progress toward your savings goals.

7. Prioritize High-Interest Debt Repayment:

High-interest debt can erode your financial foundation. Prioritize paying off high-interest debts to free up more money for savings. Utilize extra funds, windfalls, or bonuses to tackle outstanding debts strategically. Reducing debt not only saves on interest payments but also contributes to an overall healthier financial picture.

8. Educate Yourself About Personal Finance:

Knowledge is a powerful tool for financial empowerment. Invest time in educating yourself about personal finance principles, investment options, and savings strategies. Understand the impact of compound interest, explore different savings vehicles, and stay informed about economic trends. Financial literacy enhances your ability to make informed decisions and navigate the complexities of personal finance.

9. Establish a Savings Routine:

Consistency is key to cultivating a savings mindset. Establish a routine for reviewing your finances, setting savings goals, and tracking progress. Whether it's a monthly check-in or a quarterly financial review, a routine reinforces your commitment to financial well-being and allows for adjustments as needed.

10. Celebrate Savings Milestones:

Celebrate your achievements along the way. When you reach a savings milestone or achieve a financial goal, acknowledge your success. Recognizing and celebrating these moments reinforces positive behavior and motivates you to continue making progress.

11. Explore Tax-Advantaged Savings Options:

Take advantage of tax-advantaged savings options, such as employer-sponsored retirement plans (e.g., 401(k) or 403(b)), individual retirement accounts (IRAs), or health savings accounts (HSAs). These accounts offer tax benefits and can significantly boost your savings over time.

12. Diversify Your Savings Portfolio:

Consider diversifying your savings beyond traditional savings accounts. Explore investment options such as low-risk mutual funds, exchange-traded funds (ETFs), or individual stocks. While investments carry some level of risk, they also offer the potential for higher returns compared to traditional savings accounts.

13. Involve Family Members in Financial Planning:

If applicable, involve family members in financial discussions and planning. Cultivating a savings mindset becomes a shared goal, fostering a sense of financial responsibility among family members. Discuss financial priorities, set joint goals, and collaborate on strategies for effective money management.

14. Negotiate Expenses:

Regularly review recurring expenses and negotiate where possible. This can include negotiating bills, exploring discounts or promotions, or refinancing loans for better terms. The money saved through negotiation can be redirected toward savings goals.

15. Stay Resilient and Learn from Setbacks:

Financial journeys often involve setbacks. Unexpected expenses, economic downturns, or personal challenges can impact your savings plan. Stay resilient during tough times, learn from setbacks, and adjust your strategy as needed. A savings mindset is not about perfection but about continuous improvement and adaptability.

Cultivating a savings mindset is a holistic approach to financial well-being. It involves aligning your values with intentional financial choices, consistently saving, and staying focused on long-term goals. By integrating these strategies into your financial habits, you can create a mindset that not only prioritizes savings but also enhances your overall financial resilience and security. Remember that building a savings mindset is a gradual process, and each positive financial choice contributes to a more secure and fulfilling financial future.

Building effective saving habits is a cornerstone of financial well-being. It involves more than just setting money aside; it requires intentional strategies and a mindset shift toward prioritizing savings in your financial plan. Whether you are starting to save or looking to enhance your existing habits, adopting effective saving techniques can pave the way to financial stability and the achievement of your financial goals.

1. Set Clear and Achievable Goals:

Begin by defining your savings goals. Whether it's an emergency fund, a vacation, a down payment on a home, or retirement, clear goals provide direction and motivation. Break down larger goals into smaller, achievable milestones. Knowing what you're saving for helps create focus and discipline in your saving habits.

2. Create a Budget:

A budget is a fundamental tool for effective saving. Track your income and expenses to understand your financial inflows and outflows. Categorize your spending into fixed expenses (such as rent, utilities, and loan payments) and variable expenses (such as groceries, entertainment, and dining out). A budget helps identify areas where you can cut back and allocate more funds toward savings.

3. Pay Yourself First:

Make saving a priority by adopting the "pay yourself first" principle. Set up automatic transfers from your checking account to a designated savings account as soon as you receive your paycheck. Treating savings as a non-negotiable expense ensures that you consistently allocate funds toward your financial goals before other discretionary spending.

4. Embrace the 50/30/20 Rule:

The 50/30/20 rule is a popular budgeting guideline. Allocate 50% of your income to essentials (housing, utilities, groceries), 30% to discretionary spending (dining out, entertainment), and 20% to savings. Adjust these percentages based on your unique financial situation, but the principle of consistently saving a portion of your income remains crucial.

5. Track and Analyze Spending:

Regularly review your spending patterns to identify areas for improvement. Utilize apps or budgeting tools to track your expenses and categorize your spending. Understanding where your money goes empowers you to make informed decisions and identify opportunities for increased savings.

6. Cut Unnecessary Expenses:

Identify non-essential expenses that can be reduced or eliminated. This may include subscription services, impulse purchases, or dining out excessively. Redirect the money saved from cutting unnecessary expenses toward your savings goals. Small adjustments in spending habits can have a significant impact on your ability to save.

7. Create a Separate Savings Account:

Maintain a dedicated savings account separate from your primary checking account. This separation reduces the temptation to dip into your savings for daily expenses. Choose an account with a competitive interest rate to maximize your savings over time.

8. Take Advantage of Employer Benefits:

If your employer offers retirement savings plans or matches contributions, take full advantage of these benefits. Employer-sponsored plans, such as 401(k)s, often come with tax advantages and can significantly boost your long-term savings. Contribute at least enough to capture any employer matching contributions.

9. Start an Emergency Fund:

An emergency fund acts as a financial safety net for unexpected expenses or emergencies. Aim to save three to six months' worth of living expenses. Begin with a modest goal and gradually build your emergency fund over time. Knowing you have a financial cushion provides peace of mind and prevents reliance on credit in times of crisis.

10. Prioritize High-Interest Debt Repayment:

If you have high-interest debt, prioritize repaying it to free up more funds for savings. Tackling high-interest debt, such as credit card balances, prevents interest from accumulating and allows you to redirect those funds toward your savings goals.

11. Utilize Windfalls Wisely:

Any unexpected windfalls, such as tax refunds, work bonuses, or gifts, can significantly impact your savings. Instead of splurging on non-essential items, consider allocating a portion or the entirety of windfalls toward your savings goals. This approach accelerates your progress without impacting your regular budget.

12. Participate in Savings Challenges:

Engage in savings challenges to add an element of fun and motivation. Challenges like the "52-Week Money Challenge" or the "No-Spend Challenge" encourage disciplined saving and conscious spending. Customize these challenges to align with your financial goals and preferences.

13. Negotiate Bills and Expenses:

Regularly review recurring bills and negotiate where possible. Contact service providers to inquire about

discounts, promotions, or loyalty benefits.
Negotiating bills for utilities, insurance, or
subscriptions can result in savings that can be
redirected toward your financial goals.

14. Take Advantage of Cash Back and Rewards:

If you use credit cards responsibly, leverage cash
back and rewards programs to maximize your
savings. Choose cards that align with your spending
patterns and preferences. Accrued cash back or
rewards can be treated as additional savings or used
to offset future expenses.

15. Explore High-Yield Savings Accounts:

Consider opening a high-yield savings account to
earn more interest on your savings. These accounts
often offer higher interest rates than traditional
savings accounts, providing an opportunity to grow
your savings more rapidly.

16. Review and Adjust Regularly:

Financial situations change, and so should your
savings strategy. Regularly review your budget,

goals, and progress. Adjust your savings plan to reflect changes in income, expenses, or financial goals. Flexibility and adaptability are key to maintaining effective saving habits.

17. Involve Family Members in Saving:

If applicable, involve family members in saving decisions. Cultivate a culture of saving within your household. Discuss financial goals as a family, set joint targets, and celebrate achievements together. This collaborative approach fosters a sense of responsibility and shared financial well-being.

18. Stay Informed and Educated:

Stay informed about personal finance trends, investment opportunities, and savings strategies. Continuously educate yourself about different savings vehicles, investment options, and financial planning tools. Financial literacy empowers you to make informed decisions and optimize your savings strategy.

19. Consider Automatic Round-Ups:

Some financial institutions offer automatic round-up programs. When you make a purchase with your debit or credit card, the transaction amount is rounded up, and the difference is transferred to your savings account. This seamless process facilitates consistent saving without requiring additional effort.

20. Practice Delayed Gratification:

Cultivate the habit of delayed gratification. Before making a non-essential purchase, give yourself time to consider whether it aligns with your financial goals. Delaying immediate gratification allows you to make more intentional spending decisions and prioritize saving for the future.

Effective saving habits are fundamental to achieving financial security and realizing your financial aspirations. By incorporating these techniques into your daily life, you can build a strong foundation for long-term financial well-being. Remember that developing saving habits is a gradual process, and consistency is key. Celebrate your successes along the way, stay focused on your goals, and continually refine your savings strategy to align with your evolving financial landscape.

CHAPTER 7: Investing for the Future

Investing is a crucial aspect of financial planning that allows individuals to grow their wealth over time. There are various investment options, each with its own characteristics, risk profiles, and potential returns. Understanding these options is essential for making informed investment decisions tailored to individual financial goals and risk tolerance. Here's an introduction to various investment options:

1. Stocks:

Overview:
Stocks represent ownership in a company. When you buy a stock, you become a shareholder, owning a portion of the company's equity. Stock values can fluctuate based on the company's performance, market conditions, and economic factors.

Potential Returns:

Stocks have the potential for high returns, but they also come with higher volatility and risk. Investors can benefit from both capital appreciation (increase in stock price) and dividends (share of company profits).

Considerations:
Stock investors need to research and analyze individual companies, industry trends, and market conditions. Diversification is often recommended to spread risk across different stocks and sectors.

 2. Bonds:

Overview:
Bonds are debt securities issued by governments, municipalities, or corporations to raise capital. When you buy a bond, you are essentially lending money to the issuer in exchange for periodic interest payments and the return of the principal amount at maturity.

Potential Returns:
Bonds generally offer more predictable returns compared to stocks. The return on investment comes from interest payments and the eventual return of

the principal. Different bonds, such as government bonds and corporate bonds, carry varying levels of risk and returns.

Considerations:
Investors should consider factors such as interest rates, credit ratings, and the issuer's financial health. Bonds are often seen as a more conservative investment, suitable for capital preservation and income generation.

3. Mutual Funds:

Overview:
Mutual funds pool money from multiple investors to invest in a diversified portfolio of stocks, bonds, or other securities. Professional fund managers make investment decisions on behalf of the investors.

Potential Returns:
Mutual funds offer diversification and professional management, making them a popular choice for investors seeking exposure to a variety of assets. Returns depend on the performance of the underlying securities in the fund.

Considerations:
Investors should assess the fund's fees, historical performance, and the fund manager's strategy. There are different types of mutual funds, including equity funds, bond funds, and balanced funds, catering to various risk profiles.

4. Exchange-Traded Funds (ETFs):

Overview:
ETFs are similar to mutual funds but trade on stock exchanges like individual stocks. They typically track an index, commodity, or a basket of assets. ETFs offer diversification and liquidity.

Potential Returns:
ETF returns are linked to the performance of the underlying assets. They provide a cost-effective way for investors to gain exposure to specific sectors, industries, or asset classes without buying individual securities.

Considerations:
Investors should consider expense ratios, liquidity, and the tracking error (the difference between the ETF's performance and the index it tracks). ETFs are

known for their flexibility, allowing investors to buy and sell shares throughout the trading day.

5. Real Estate:

Overview:
Real estate involves purchasing physical properties, such as residential or commercial buildings, land, or real estate investment trusts (REITs). REITs are companies that own, operate, or finance income-generating real estate.

Potential Returns:
Real estate investments can generate rental income and capital appreciation. REITs offer a way to invest in real estate without directly owning properties. The potential for long-term growth and diversification makes real estate attractive to many investors.

Considerations:
Real estate requires significant capital and involves ongoing management responsibilities. Investors should assess location, market trends, and the potential for rental income. REIT investors should evaluate the trust's performance and dividend yield.

6. Cryptocurrencies:

Overview:
Cryptocurrencies, such as Bitcoin and Ethereum, are digital or virtual currencies that use cryptography for security. They operate on decentralized blockchain technology and are not controlled by any central authority.

Potential Returns:
Cryptocurrencies have gained attention for their potential high returns but come with significant volatility and risk. Investors can profit from price appreciation or engage in cryptocurrency trading.

Considerations:
Investing in cryptocurrencies requires a strong understanding of the technology, market dynamics, and regulatory landscape. Due to their speculative nature, cryptocurrencies should be approached with caution, and investors should be prepared for price fluctuations.

7. Retirement Accounts:

Overview:
Retirement accounts, such as 401(k)s and IRAs, offer tax advantages to encourage long-term savings for retirement. These accounts can hold various investments, including stocks, bonds, and mutual funds.

Potential Returns:
Returns in retirement accounts are influenced by the performance of the chosen investments. Contributions to these accounts are often tax-deductible or may provide tax-free withdrawals in retirement, depending on the type of account.

Considerations:
Investors should consider factors such as contribution limits, withdrawal penalties, and the tax implications of different retirement accounts. Retirement accounts are designed for long-term savings and may have restrictions on early withdrawals.

 8. Savings Accounts:

Overview:

Savings accounts are low-risk deposit accounts offered by banks or credit unions. They provide a safe place to store money while earning interest. However, interest rates on savings accounts are generally lower than potential returns from other investments.

Potential Returns:
Returns from savings accounts come in the form of interest, and they are often considered a conservative option for preserving capital. While the returns may be modest, savings accounts offer liquidity and safety.

Considerations:
Savings accounts are suitable for short-term goals and emergency funds. Investors should be aware of interest rates, fees, and any withdrawal restrictions imposed by the financial institution.

9. Gold and Precious Metals:

Overview:
Investing in precious metals, such as gold and silver, is a hedge against inflation and economic uncertainty. Investors can buy physical metals,

exchange-traded funds (ETFs), or shares in mining
companies.

Potential Returns:
Precious metals can provide a store of value and
may appreciate during times of economic
uncertainty. Their value is influenced by factors
such as supply and demand, geopolitical events, and
inflation.

Considerations:
Investors should carefully evaluate the reasons for
investing in precious metals and consider the
associated costs, storage, and liquidity. Precious
metals can serve as a diversification tool within an
investment portfolio.

10. Certificates of Deposit (CDs):

Overview:
Certificates of Deposit (CDs) are time deposits
offered by banks with a fixed term and interest rate.
Investors deposit a specific amount for a
predetermined period, and in return, they receive the
principal plus interest at maturity.

Potential Returns:
CDs provide a fixed interest rate, making them a predictable and low-risk investment. However, returns may be lower compared to riskier assets. Early withdrawals may result in penalties.

Considerations:
CDs are suitable for investors seeking capital preservation and a guaranteed return. The fixed term requires careful consideration of liquidity needs. Investors can ladder CDs with different maturity dates for flexibility.

Each investment option comes with its own set of risks, returns, and considerations. Building a diversified investment portfolio often involves a combination of these options based on individual financial goals, risk tolerance, and time horizon. A well-rounded investment strategy typically includes a mix of asset classes to balance risk and potential returns. Here are additional considerations and tips for navigating the diverse landscape of investment options:

Diversification:

Diversification is a key principle in investment strategy. By spreading investments across different asset classes, sectors, and geographical regions, investors can mitigate the impact of poor performance in any single investment. Diversification reduces the overall risk of a portfolio and enhances the potential for stable, long-term returns.

Risk Tolerance:

Understanding your risk tolerance is crucial in building an investment portfolio. Different investment options carry varying levels of risk, and individuals may have different comfort levels with market fluctuations. Assess your willingness and ability to tolerate risk, and align your investments accordingly. Riskier assets may offer higher potential returns but come with increased volatility.

Time Horizon:

Consider your investment time horizon—the length of time you plan to hold your investments before needing to access the funds. Longer time horizons may allow for a more aggressive investment approach, taking advantage of compounding returns. Shorter time horizons may warrant a more conservative strategy to protect capital and ensure liquidity when needed.

Research and Due Diligence:

Thorough research and due diligence are essential before making any investment decisions. Understand the characteristics, historical performance, and potential risks of each investment option. Stay informed about market trends, economic indicators, and relevant news that may impact your investments. For individual stocks or bonds, analyze company financials and industry trends.

Costs and Fees:

Be mindful of the costs associated with each investment option. Different investments come with various fees, such as expense ratios for mutual funds and ETFs, transaction fees for stock trades, or management fees for certain financial products. Minimizing costs is crucial to maximizing overall returns. Compare fees across similar investment options and choose cost-effective solutions.

Rebalancing:

Regularly reassess and rebalance your investment portfolio. Over time, market fluctuations may cause the original asset allocation to shift. Periodically review your portfolio, adjust allocations based on changes in your financial situation or market conditions, and rebalance to maintain the desired risk profile.

Professional Advice:

Consider seeking advice from financial professionals, such as certified financial planners or investment advisors. Professionals can provide personalized guidance based on your individual financial goals and circumstances. They can help tailor an investment strategy, assess risk, and navigate complex financial markets.

Stay Informed About Economic Conditions:

Keep yourself informed about broader economic conditions and global events that may impact financial markets. Economic indicators, interest rates, inflation rates, and geopolitical events can influence the performance of various investments. Staying informed enables you to make proactive decisions and adjust your investment strategy when needed.

Emergency Fund:

Before diving into investments, ensure you have an emergency fund. An emergency fund provides a financial safety net for unexpected expenses or disruptions in income. Having a readily accessible cash reserve prevents the need to liquidate investments during times of urgency, allowing your long-term investments to remain intact.

Regularly Monitor and Evaluate:

Investing is an ongoing process that requires regular monitoring and evaluation. Review your investment portfolio periodically to assess its performance, alignment with financial goals, and overall suitability. Adjustments may be necessary based on changes in personal circumstances or shifts in the economic landscape.

Behavioral Considerations:

Understand your own behavioral tendencies and emotions related to investing. Emotional decisions, driven by fear or greed, can lead to suboptimal outcomes. Stick to your investment strategy and resist the temptation to make impulsive decisions based on short-term market movements.

Educational Resources:

Continue to educate yourself about investing principles and financial markets. Numerous educational resources, including books, articles, and online courses, provide valuable insights into various investment options, strategies, and market dynamics. Strengthening your financial literacy empowers you to make informed decisions and navigate the complexities of investing.

Investing is a dynamic and personalized journey that requires careful consideration, research, and ongoing attention. By understanding the characteristics of different investment options and aligning them with your financial goals, risk tolerance, and time horizon, you can build a diversified portfolio that positions you for long-term success. Continuously evaluate your investments, stay informed about market conditions, and, if needed, seek professional advice to optimize your investment strategy. Remember that investing is a long-term endeavor, and patience, discipline, and informed decision-making are key components of a successful investment approach.

Building a well-structured investment portfolio is a strategic process that involves careful consideration of various factors, including financial goals, risk tolerance, and time horizon. An effective investment portfolio is diversified, aligns with individual objectives, and adapts to changing market conditions. Here's a comprehensive guide to creating an investment portfolio:

1. Define Your Financial Goals:

Before constructing a portfolio, clearly articulate your financial goals. Whether it's saving for a home, funding education, or retirement planning, each goal may have a different time horizon and risk tolerance. Understanding your objectives will guide the selection of appropriate investments.

2. Assess Your Risk Tolerance:

Evaluate your risk tolerance, which reflects your comfort level with the potential for investment fluctuations. Risk tolerance is influenced by factors such as age, financial stability, and psychological willingness to accept market volatility. A risk assessment can help determine an appropriate asset allocation.

3. Determine Your Time Horizon:

Your time horizon, or the anticipated length of time your investments will be held, is a critical factor in portfolio construction. Longer time horizons may allow for a more aggressive strategy with a higher allocation to equities, while shorter time horizons may warrant a more conservative approach.

4. Asset Allocation:

Asset allocation is the distribution of your investment portfolio across different asset classes, such as stocks, bonds, and alternative investments. The goal is to create a balanced mix that aligns with your risk tolerance and financial goals. Common asset allocation strategies include:

- Conservative Portfolio: Emphasizes capital preservation and income generation, with a higher allocation to bonds and cash.

- Balanced Portfolio: Aims for a mix of growth and income by combining stocks and bonds in varying proportions.

- Aggressive Portfolio: Prioritizes capital appreciation with a higher allocation to stocks, potentially offering higher returns but accompanied by increased volatility.

5. Diversification:

Diversification is a key risk management strategy. Spread your investments across different industries, sectors, and geographical regions to reduce the impact of poor performance in any single asset.

Diversification enhances the potential for stable, long-term returns by mitigating concentration risk.

 6. Selecting Investments:

Once you've determined your asset allocation, select specific investments within each asset class. Consider factors such as:

- Equities (Stocks): Choose individual stocks, mutual funds, or exchange-traded funds (ETFs) based on your risk tolerance and investment goals. Research individual companies or opt for diversified funds.

- Bonds: Evaluate government bonds, corporate bonds, or municipal bonds. Consider factors like credit ratings, interest rates, and maturity dates.

- Real Estate: Explore real estate investment trusts (REITs) or direct real estate investments to add a tangible asset class to your portfolio.

- Alternative Investments: Include alternative investments, such as commodities, precious metals, or private equity, for additional diversification.

7. Review and Rebalance:

Regularly review your portfolio to ensure it aligns with your goals and risk tolerance. Market fluctuations may cause your asset allocation to deviate from the original plan. Rebalance the portfolio by buying or selling assets to bring it back in line with your desired allocation.

8. Consider Tax Implications:

Understand the tax implications of your investments. Utilize tax-advantaged accounts such as IRAs or 401(k)s for retirement savings. Consider tax-efficient investment strategies to minimize the impact of taxes on your returns.

9. Stay Informed:

Keep yourself informed about market trends, economic indicators, and global events that may impact your investments. Regularly assess the performance of your investments and be prepared to adjust your strategy based on changing market conditions.

10. Emergency Fund:

Before focusing on investments, ensure you have an emergency fund. An emergency fund provides a financial safety net for unexpected expenses, preventing the need to liquidate investments during times of urgency.

11. Dollar-Cost Averaging:

Consider employing a dollar-cost averaging strategy, where you consistently invest a fixed amount at regular intervals regardless of market conditions. This approach can reduce the impact of market volatility on your overall investment performance.

12. Reinvestment of Dividends:

Reinvest dividends to maximize the compounding effect of your investments. Many stocks and funds offer the option to automatically reinvest dividends, allowing you to acquire additional shares over time.

13. Seek Professional Advice:

If you're unsure about constructing your portfolio, consider seeking advice from financial professionals. Certified financial planners or investment advisors can provide personalized guidance based on your individual financial situation and goals.

Example Portfolio Allocations:

1. Conservative Portfolio (For Capital Preservation):
    - 40% Bonds (Government and Corporate)
    - 30% Cash or Money Market
    - 20% Blue-Chip Stocks
    - 10% Real Estate Investment Trusts (REITs)

2. Balanced Portfolio (For Growth and Income):
    - 50% Equities (Diversified Stocks or ETFs)
    - 30% Bonds (Mix of Government and Corporate)
    - 15% Real Estate (REITs)
    - 5% Alternative Investments (Precious Metals or Commodities)

3. Aggressive Portfolio (For Capital Appreciation):
    - 70% Equities (Diversified Stocks or ETFs)
    - 20% High-Yield Corporate Bonds
    - 5% Real Estate (Direct or REITs)

- 5% Alternative Investments (Private Equity or Cryptocurrencies)

Constructing an investment portfolio is a dynamic process that requires thoughtful planning, ongoing evaluation, and adaptability. By aligning your portfolio with your financial goals, risk tolerance, and time horizon, you can create a diversified strategy that maximizes the potential for long-term returns while managing risk. Regularly reassess and adjust your portfolio as needed, staying informed about market conditions and seeking professional advice when necessary. Remember that investing is a journey, and a well-constructed portfolio serves as a roadmap to financial success.

CHAPTER 8: Navigating Risks

Risk assessment plays a pivotal role in making informed financial decisions. Whether investing, borrowing, or managing day-to-day finances, understanding and evaluating risks is essential for achieving financial goals and safeguarding economic well-being. This comprehensive guide explores the significance of risk assessment in various financial decisions.

1. Understanding Risk:

Risk in the financial context refers to the uncertainty associated with an investment or financial decision. It encompasses the possibility of losing money, not achieving expected returns, or facing adverse consequences due to unforeseen events. Different types of risks exist, including market risk, credit risk, liquidity risk, and operational risk.

2. Types of Financial Risks:

- Market Risk: Arises from fluctuations in financial markets. For example, changes in interest rates, stock prices, or commodity prices can impact the value of investments.

- Credit Risk: The risk of default by a borrower. This is relevant when lending money or investing in bonds. A borrower may fail to repay a loan or interest, leading to financial losses.

- Liquidity Risk: The risk of not being able to quickly convert an investment into cash without a significant loss. Illiquid assets may be challenging to sell at desired prices.

- Operational Risk: Relates to the risk of loss from inadequate internal processes, systems, human error, or external events. It can impact a company's financial stability.

- Inflation Risk: The risk that the purchasing power of money will decline due to inflation. Investments may not keep pace with rising prices, leading to reduced real returns.

 3. Significance of Risk Assessment:

- Informed Decision-Making: Risk assessment provides the information needed to make well-informed decisions. By understanding potential risks, individuals and businesses can weigh the potential rewards against the likelihood of adverse outcomes.

- Goal Alignment: Different financial goals come with varying risk tolerances. Risk assessment helps align investment strategies with specific objectives, ensuring that the chosen level of risk corresponds with the desired outcomes.

- Portfolio Diversification: Diversifying investments across different asset classes is a risk management strategy. Risk assessment aids in creating a diversified portfolio that balances risk and potential returns.

- Financial Stability: Assessing risks is crucial for maintaining financial stability. It helps identify potential threats and implement strategies to mitigate or manage those risks, reducing the likelihood of financial setbacks.

4. Risk Tolerance:

Risk tolerance refers to an individual's or an entity's ability and willingness to withstand fluctuations in the value of their investments. Factors influencing risk tolerance include:

- Financial Situation: Individuals with stable financial situations may have higher risk tolerance, while those facing financial challenges may prefer lower-risk investments.

- Investment Goals: Short-term goals may warrant a lower risk tolerance to preserve capital, while long-term goals may allow for higher-risk investments with the potential for greater returns.

- Time Horizon: Longer time horizons may afford the luxury of waiting out market fluctuations, influencing a higher risk tolerance.

5. Risk Management Strategies:

- Diversification: Spreading investments across different asset classes and geographic regions can mitigate the impact of poor performance in any single investment.

- Asset Allocation: Balancing the distribution of investments between equities, bonds, and other assets based on risk tolerance and financial goals.

- Insurance: Using insurance products to protect against specific risks, such as health, property, or life insurance.

- Emergency Funds: Maintaining an emergency fund provides a financial buffer to cope with unforeseen expenses or income disruptions.

- Risk Mitigation Plans: Creating plans to address specific risks, such as implementing hedging strategies in investments or developing contingency plans for business operations.

6. Risk Assessment in Investing:

- Research and Due Diligence: Thoroughly researching potential investments and conducting due diligence is a fundamental aspect of risk assessment. Understanding a company's financial health, industry trends, and market conditions helps evaluate potential risks.

- Financial Ratios: Utilizing financial ratios, such as debt-to-equity ratio, return on investment, and volatility measures, provides insights into the risk profile of an investment.

- Historical Performance: Analyzing historical performance helps identify patterns and assess how an investment has responded to different market conditions.

- Economic Indicators: Monitoring economic indicators, interest rates, and geopolitical events provides context for potential market movements and helps anticipate risks.

7. Risk Assessment in Borrowing:

- Credit Scores: Lenders assess borrowers' creditworthiness through credit scores. Individuals with higher credit scores are deemed lower risk, leading to favorable loan terms.

- Interest Rates: The interest rate on a loan reflects the perceived risk. Higher-risk borrowers may face higher interest rates to compensate lenders for the increased likelihood of default.

- Collateral: Providing collateral can mitigate credit risk for lenders. It serves as security, allowing them to recover some value in case of default.

8. Risk Assessment in Business Operations:

- Supply Chain Risk: Assessing the reliability and stability of the supply chain helps mitigate disruptions due to factors like natural disasters, geopolitical events, or supplier insolvency.

- Operational Efficiency: Evaluating internal processes and systems helps identify vulnerabilities and implement improvements to enhance operational efficiency and reduce the risk of errors.

- Regulatory Compliance: Staying compliant with regulations relevant to the industry mitigates legal and regulatory risks that could result in fines or legal consequences.

9. Behavioral Finance and Risk:

- Emotional Bias: Understanding behavioral biases, such as fear and greed, is crucial. Emotional decision-making can lead to impulsive actions that may not align with a well-thought-out risk strategy.

- Loss Aversion: Investors often have a greater aversion to losses than the joy derived from equivalent gains. Recognizing and managing loss aversion is essential for rational decision-making.

10. Risk Communication:

Effective communication of risks is vital for transparent decision-making, whether in personal finances, investing, or business operations. Clear communication ensures that all stakeholders are aware of potential risks and can actively participate in risk management strategies.

Risk assessment is an integral aspect of financial decision-making, influencing strategies for investments, borrowing, and business operations. Understanding and managing risks is not about avoiding them entirely but about making informed choices that align with specific goals and circumstances. It involves a dynamic process of continuous evaluation, adaptation, and mitigation.

In conclusion, individuals, investors, and businesses must recognize that risk is inherent in all financial decisions. However, the key lies in proactively assessing, managing, and sometimes embracing these risks to achieve financial success and resilience. Developing a robust risk management strategy involves a combination of informed decision-making, diversification, and a clear understanding of risk tolerance.

Financial decisions should be guided by a thoughtful consideration of short-term and long-term goals, with risk assessment serving as a compass for navigating the complex landscape of uncertainties. By acknowledging the multifaceted nature of risk and incorporating risk management into financial planning, individuals and entities can enhance their ability to weather challenges, capitalize on opportunities, and ultimately achieve sustainable financial well-being. Remember that a well-informed and balanced approach to risk is a cornerstone of sound financial stewardship.

Mitigating and managing financial risks is a critical aspect of sound financial planning for individuals, businesses, and investors. Financial risks can arise from various sources, including market volatility, economic uncertainties, credit challenges, and operational vulnerabilities. This comprehensive guide explores key strategies for identifying, mitigating, and managing financial risks effectively.

1. Risk Identification:

The first step in managing financial risks is to identify and understand the potential threats. This involves a thorough assessment of various risk factors, including market risks, credit risks, liquidity risks, operational risks, and external factors such as geopolitical events or regulatory changes.

- Scenario Analysis: Conducting scenario analysis involves evaluating how different events or changes in market conditions could impact financial outcomes. This proactive approach helps anticipate potential risks and develop strategies to address them.

- Regular Risk Assessments: Periodic reviews of financial positions, investment portfolios, and business operations are essential for staying informed about changing risk profiles. Regular risk assessments allow for timely adjustments to risk management strategies.

2. Diversification:

Diversification is a fundamental risk management strategy that involves spreading investments or business activities across different assets, industries, or markets. This approach aims to reduce the impact of poor performance in any single investment or business segment.

- Investment Diversification: For investors, diversifying a portfolio involves holding a mix of asset classes such as stocks, bonds, real estate, and alternative investments. This helps balance risk and potential returns.

- Business Diversification: Businesses can diversify their product or service offerings, target markets, or supply chains. Diversification can provide stability by minimizing reliance on a single revenue stream or customer base.

3. Insurance Protection:

Insurance is a crucial tool for mitigating financial risks by transferring certain risks to an insurance provider. Different types of insurance can provide protection against specific risks:

- Health Insurance: Covers medical expenses and mitigates the financial impact of unexpected healthcare costs.

- Property and Casualty Insurance: Protects against damages to property and liability risks.

- Life Insurance: Provides financial support to beneficiaries in the event of the policyholder's death.

- Business Interruption Insurance: Helps businesses recover financial losses due to disruptions, such as natural disasters or unforeseen events.

4. Emergency Funds:

Maintaining an emergency fund is a personal finance strategy that acts as a financial cushion in times of unexpected expenses or income disruptions. An emergency fund serves as a safety net, reducing the need to liquidate investments or rely on credit during challenging times.

- Size of Emergency Fund: The size of an emergency fund should cover essential living expenses for a recommended period, typically three to six months. This ensures financial stability during unexpected circumstances like job loss or medical emergencies.

5. Effective Cash Management:

Efficient cash management is essential for individuals and businesses alike. Proper cash flow management helps ensure that there is enough liquidity to cover immediate expenses, debts, and capital requirements.

- Cash Flow Forecasting: Regularly forecasting cash flows enables proactive planning and helps identify potential cash shortages or surpluses.

- Working Capital Management: For businesses, optimizing working capital by managing accounts receivable, inventory, and accounts payable is crucial for maintaining liquidity.

6. Due Diligence in Investments:

Conducting thorough due diligence before making investment decisions is paramount to managing investment risks. Whether investing in stocks, bonds, real estate, or other assets, due diligence involves:

- Company and Industry Analysis: Understanding the financial health of a company and its industry dynamics helps assess the potential risks and rewards of an investment.

- Risk-Reward Assessment: Evaluating the risk-return profile of an investment ensures alignment with the investor's risk tolerance and financial goals.

- Legal and Regulatory Compliance: Ensuring that investments comply with relevant laws and regulations helps mitigate legal and regulatory risks.

7. Risk Mitigation Plans:

Developing specific risk mitigation plans is crucial for addressing identified risks. These plans outline strategies and actions to minimize the impact of potential threats and ensure continuity.

- Contingency Plans: Contingency plans outline steps to be taken in response to specific events, such as natural disasters, economic downturns, or operational disruptions.

- Hedging Strategies: Financial instruments, such as options or futures contracts, can be employed to hedge against certain risks, particularly in volatile markets or for businesses exposed to commodity price fluctuations.

8. Credit Risk Management:

Credit risk is prevalent in lending and financial transactions. Managing credit risk involves assessing the creditworthiness of borrowers and implementing strategies to minimize the likelihood of default.

- Credit Scoring: Utilizing credit scores helps lenders evaluate the creditworthiness of individuals and businesses. Higher credit scores indicate lower credit risk.

- Collateral and Security: Securing loans with collateral or guarantees reduces credit risk for lenders. In case of default, lenders can recover part of their losses by seizing the collateral.

9. Market Risk Mitigation:

Market risks, such as fluctuations in interest rates or stock prices, can impact investment portfolios and financial stability. Mitigating market risks involves strategic planning and diversified investment approaches.

- Asset Allocation: Balancing the allocation of assets in a portfolio based on risk tolerance and market conditions helps manage exposure to market volatility.

- Derivatives and Options: Strategic use of derivatives or options can provide a level of protection against adverse market movements.

10. Operational Risk Management:

Operational risks arise from internal processes, systems, or external events that can disrupt business operations. Effectively managing operational risks involves:

- Internal Controls: Implementing robust internal controls and procedures to minimize the risk of errors, fraud, or operational failures.

- Employee Training: Educating employees on risk management protocols and ensuring they are well-equipped to handle operational challenges.

11. Technology and Cybersecurity Measures:

As technology plays an increasingly significant role in financial transactions and business operations, managing cybersecurity risks is essential. This includes safeguarding sensitive data, implementing encryption, and regularly updating cybersecurity measures.

- Data Protection: Employing data encryption, secure networks, and regular audits to protect against data breaches and unauthorized access.

- Cybersecurity Training: Providing employees with training on cybersecurity best practices to reduce the risk of phishing attacks or other cyber threats.

12. Regulatory Compliance:

Compliance with relevant laws and regulations is crucial for managing legal and regulatory risks. Failure to comply with regulations can result in financial penalties, legal consequences, and damage to reputation.

- Regular Compliance Audits: Conducting regular audits to ensure adherence to changing regulations and promptly addressing any compliance issues that arise.

- Legal Counsel: Seeking legal advice to stay informed about regulatory changes and to address legal risks associated with business operations.

13. Monitoring and Review:

Ongoing monitoring and regular reviews of risk management strategies are essential for adapting to changing circumstances and staying ahead of emerging risks.

- Performance Metrics: Establishing key performance indicators (KPIs) to measure the effectiveness of risk management strategies and making adjustments as needed.

- Periodic Reviews: Conducting periodic reviews of risk management plans, adjusting strategies based on changing market conditions, and incorporating lessons learned from past experiences.

Effectively mitigating and managing financial risks requires a proactive and multifaceted approach. Whether at the individual, business, or investment level, a robust risk management strategy involves continuous evaluation, strategic planning, and adaptability. By identifying potential risks, implementing mitigation measures, and staying vigilant in monitoring financial positions, individuals and entities can navigate uncertainties, protect assets, and work towards achieving sustainable financial success. Remember, a well-executed risk management strategy is not just a safeguard against potential threats but also a cornerstone for building resilience and seizing opportunities in an ever-evolving financial landscape.

CHAPTER 9: Financial Independence Milestones

Celebrating small victories is an essential and often overlooked aspect of personal development and well-being. In a world that often emphasizes grand achievements and monumental milestones, recognizing and appreciating small wins can have profound positive effects on mental health, motivation, and overall life satisfaction. This guide delves into the significance of celebrating small victories, strategies for doing so, and the far-reaching impact on individual growth and happiness.

1. The Power of Small Victories:

- Psychological Boost: Small victories, even seemingly insignificant ones, provide a psychological boost by activating the brain's reward system. This can lead to increased levels of dopamine, the "feel-good" neurotransmitter, promoting a sense of accomplishment and happiness.

- Motivation Catalyst: Celebrating small wins acts as a catalyst for motivation. Accomplishing minor tasks creates a positive momentum that can spill over into tackling more significant challenges, fostering a proactive and achievement-oriented mindset.

- Building Confidence: Regular acknowledgment of small victories contributes to building self-confidence. Each acknowledgment reinforces the belief that one is capable of overcoming challenges, which can be particularly beneficial during larger endeavors.

- Cultivating Resilience: Small victories play a vital role in cultivating resilience. They teach individuals to bounce back from setbacks, learn from experiences, and approach challenges with a positive and solution-oriented mindset.

2. Strategies for Celebrating Small Victories:

- Mindful Reflection: Take time for mindful reflection on daily achievements. Whether it's completing a task, reaching a personal goal, or overcoming a challenge, consciously acknowledging these accomplishments is the first step in celebrating small victories.

- Gratitude Practice: Cultivate a gratitude practice by expressing thanks for the small positive aspects of each day. This can be done through journaling, verbally acknowledging gratitude, or simply taking a moment to appreciate the positives.

- Reward System: Implement a personal reward system for achieving small goals. This can be as simple as treating yourself to a favorite snack, enjoying a leisure activity, or taking a short break to relax and recharge.

- Share Achievements: Share your small victories with friends, family, or colleagues. Verbalizing accomplishments not only reinforces their significance but also allows for social validation and support.

3. The Impact on Mental Health:

- Reducing Stress: Celebrating small victories contributes to stress reduction. It shifts the focus from overwhelming long-term goals to manageable, achievable tasks, promoting a more positive and less stressful mindset.

- Enhancing Well-being: Regularly acknowledging small wins enhances overall well-being. It fosters a sense of accomplishment, satisfaction, and contentment, contributing to a more positive outlook on life.

- Managing Anxiety: Small victories provide a sense of control, which is particularly valuable in managing anxiety. Breaking down larger tasks into smaller, more manageable steps can alleviate feelings of overwhelm.

- Boosting Self-Esteem: The cumulative effect of celebrating small victories significantly boosts self-esteem. It reinforces the notion that one is capable and competent, instilling a positive self-image.

4. Relationship Dynamics:

- Building Team Morale: In a team or professional setting, recognizing and celebrating small victories can significantly boost team morale. It creates a positive and supportive work environment, fostering collaboration and camaraderie.

- Family Bonding: Celebrating small victories within a family strengthens bonds. Whether it's a child's academic achievement, a shared accomplishment, or overcoming a family challenge, these celebrations create lasting positive memories.

- Cultivating Support Networks: Sharing successes with friends or support groups strengthens relationships. It allows individuals to celebrate one another's achievements, creating a network of encouragement and shared joy.

5. Navigating Setbacks:

- Learning Opportunities: Small victories often come with lessons, even in setbacks. Celebrating the effort and acknowledging what was learned in the face of challenges turns setbacks into opportunities for growth.

- Maintaining Perspective: In the face of setbacks, celebrating small victories maintains perspective. It prevents individuals from becoming discouraged by setbacks and helps them focus on the progress made, no matter how small.

 6. Balancing Ambition and Contentment:

- Promoting a Growth Mindset: Celebrating small victories aligns with a growth mindset. It encourages the belief that abilities can be developed through dedication and hard work, fostering a continuous desire for improvement.

- Preventing Burnout: Constantly striving for significant achievements without celebrating small victories can lead to burnout. Recognizing and appreciating incremental progress provides a sense of balance and prevents exhaustion.

- Cultivating Contentment: Regularly celebrating small victories cultivates contentment. It teaches individuals to find joy in the journey rather than exclusively focusing on distant, often elusive, destinations.

7. In Professional Settings:

- Employee Engagement: Recognizing and celebrating small victories in the workplace boosts employee engagement. It fosters a positive company culture and encourages employees to take pride in their work.

- Productivity Enhancement: Acknowledging small wins contributes to increased productivity. Employees are motivated to tackle tasks with enthusiasm when they feel their efforts are valued and recognized.

- Strengthening Team Dynamics: In team environments, celebrating small victories strengthens team dynamics. It promotes collaboration, mutual support, and a shared sense of achievement.

8. Long-Term Impact on Goal Attainment:

- Sustainable Progress: Consistently celebrating small victories contributes to sustainable progress. It prevents burnout, keeps individuals motivated, and sustains momentum over the long term.

- Goal Reinforcement: Celebrating small victories reinforces the pursuit of larger goals. It creates positive associations with the journey, making individuals more likely to persevere through challenges.

- Positive Habits: The habit of celebrating small victories contributes to the development of positive habits. It establishes a framework for recognizing achievements, reinforcing a mindset of success and progress.

Celebrating small victories is not just about acknowledging accomplishments; it's a transformative practice that positively impacts mental health, motivation, relationships, and long-term goal attainment. By embracing the power of small wins, individuals can foster resilience, build confidence, and create a life filled with a sense of accomplishment and joy. In a world often fixated on major milestones, the art of celebrating small victories is a powerful reminder that every step forward, no matter how small, is a meaningful and worthy achievement.

Tracking progress toward financial goals is a fundamental aspect of effective financial planning. Whether aiming for short-term objectives like building an emergency fund or long-term goals such as retirement planning, monitoring and assessing progress is crucial for staying on course. This guide explores the significance of tracking financial goals, strategies for effective monitoring, and the positive impact it can have on overall financial well-being.

1. The Importance of Goal Tracking:

- Clarity and Focus: Regularly tracking financial goals provides clarity and helps maintain focus. It ensures that individuals and households have a clear understanding of what they are working toward and why.

- Motivation: Tracking progress serves as a powerful motivator. Seeing tangible advancements, even small ones, can boost motivation and reinforce the commitment to achieving financial goals.

- Adaptability: Life is dynamic, and circumstances change. Tracking financial goals allows for adaptability. It enables individuals to adjust their strategies in response to changes in income, expenses, or unforeseen events.

- Financial Awareness: Regular goal tracking fosters financial awareness. It encourages individuals to be mindful of their spending habits, savings patterns, and investment decisions, promoting overall financial literacy.

2. Setting SMART Financial Goals:

- Specific: Goals should be specific and clearly defined. Instead of a vague goal like "save money," a specific goal would be "save $5,000 for an emergency fund."

- Measurable: Goals should be measurable to track progress effectively. For instance, a measurable goal could be "pay off $10,000 in credit card debt within 12 months."

- Achievable: Goals should be realistic and attainable. Setting goals that are too ambitious may lead to frustration, while achievable goals encourage sustained effort.

- Relevant: Goals should be relevant to an individual's overall financial plan and life circumstances. Aligning financial goals with personal values ensures greater commitment.

- Time-Bound: Goals should have a timeline for completion. Establishing a deadline creates a sense of urgency and helps in planning the necessary steps to achieve the goal within the specified timeframe.

 3. Creating a Financial Plan:

- Budgeting: A well-crafted budget is essential for effective goal tracking. It provides a detailed breakdown of income, expenses, and savings, serving as a roadmap for financial success.

- Emergency Fund: Building an emergency fund is a foundational financial goal. Having a safety net ensures financial resilience and prevents the need to dip into long-term savings for unexpected expenses.

- Debt Repayment Plan: For those with outstanding debts, creating a debt repayment plan is crucial. Prioritizing high-interest debt and systematically paying it down accelerates progress toward financial freedom.

- Investment Strategy: Whether saving for retirement, education, or other long-term goals, a strategic investment plan is essential. Regularly contributing to investment accounts and adjusting allocations based on risk tolerance and market conditions is key.

 4. Utilizing Financial Tools:

- Personal Finance Apps: Numerous personal finance apps are available to help track spending, savings, and progress toward financial goals. These apps often provide visual representations of financial data for easy understanding.

- Spreadsheets: Creating a simple spreadsheet is an effective way to manually track financial goals. Excel or Google Sheets can be customized to include income, expenses, savings, and progress toward specific goals.

- Automated Tracking Systems: Many banks and financial institutions offer automated tracking systems. These tools categorize spending, provide insights into saving patterns, and offer a holistic view of financial health.

5. Regularly Monitoring Progress:

- Monthly Check-Ins: Schedule monthly check-ins to review financial goals. This regular cadence allows for timely adjustments and ensures that individuals stay on top of their financial objectives.

- Comparing Actual vs. Planned: Compare actual financial outcomes with the planned budget and savings targets. Analyzing any variances helps identify areas for improvement and reinforces responsible financial habits.

- Celebrate Achievements: Take the time to celebrate achievements, no matter how small. Acknowledging progress fosters a positive mindset and motivates continued commitment to financial goals.

6. Adjusting Strategies When Needed:

- Life Changes: Life events such as job changes, marriage, or the birth of a child may necessitate adjustments to financial goals. Being flexible and recalibrating goals in response to significant life changes is essential.

- Economic Conditions: Economic conditions can impact income, expenses, and investment returns. Monitoring economic trends and adjusting financial strategies accordingly ensures resilience in the face of external factors.

- Emergency Situations: Unforeseen emergencies may arise, requiring individuals to temporarily redirect funds or reassess priorities. Having a plan for dealing with unexpected situations is integral to successful financial goal tracking.

7. Addressing Setbacks:

- Learn from Setbacks: Financial setbacks are part of the journey. Instead of viewing setbacks as failures, use them as learning opportunities. Identify the root causes, adjust strategies, and continue moving forward.

- Reassessing Goals: In the face of significant setbacks, reassessing goals may be necessary. It's okay to modify timelines or adjust expectations to better align with current circumstances.

 8. The Psychological Impact:

- Reducing Stress: Consistently tracking and making progress toward financial goals reduces financial stress. It creates a sense of control over one's financial situation, contributing to overall well-being.

- Boosting Confidence: Achieving financial milestones, no matter how small, boosts confidence. This newfound confidence extends beyond financial matters, positively impacting various aspects of an individual's life.

- Enhancing Quality of Life: Successful goal tracking enhances the quality of life. It allows individuals to allocate resources efficiently, pursue experiences that matter, and build a foundation for long-term financial security.

9. Long-Term Financial Success:

- Consistency is Key: Long-term financial success is built on consistency. Regularly tracking goals, making adjustments when necessary, and staying committed to the financial plan contribute to sustained success.

- Adapting to Life Stages: As life stages change, financial goals evolve. Adapting to these changes, whether transitioning to retirement or saving for a child's education, ensures that financial plans remain relevant and effective.

- Legacy Planning: Long-term financial success includes legacy planning. This may involve estate planning, creating a will, or establishing trusts to safeguard assets and provide for future generations.

Tracking progress toward financial goals is a dynamic and ongoing process that requires commitment, adaptability, and a strategic approach. Whether aiming for short-term financial stability or long-term wealth accumulation, consistent monitoring ensures that individuals stay on course and make informed decisions. The positive impact goes beyond financial metrics, influencing overall well-being, reducing stress, and fostering a sense of control over one's financial destiny. By embracing the discipline of goal tracking, individuals can navigate life's financial complexities with confidence, resilience, and the assurance of a secure financial future.

CHAPTER 10: Generational Wealth

Passing on financial knowledge is a transformative and empowering endeavor. Whether teaching family members, friends, or a wider community, the impact of imparting financial wisdom can shape individuals' futures and contribute to broader economic well-being. This guide explores the importance of sharing financial knowledge, effective strategies for doing so, and the long-lasting benefits it can bring to individuals and society.

1. The Importance of Financial Education:

- Empowerment: Financial knowledge empowers individuals to make informed decisions about money, budgeting, investing, and overall financial planning. This empowerment fosters a sense of control and confidence in managing one's financial life.

- Lifelong Skills: Financial education provides individuals with lifelong skills. From basic budgeting to understanding complex investment strategies, the knowledge gained becomes a valuable asset that can be applied in various life stages.

- Breaking Cycles: Access to financial education has the potential to break generational cycles of financial instability. By equipping individuals with the skills to manage money effectively, they can create a foundation for improved financial well-being for themselves and future generations.

2. Identifying the Audience:

- Tailoring Approach: Recognize the diverse needs and backgrounds of the audience. Whether teaching children, young adults, or older individuals, tailoring the approach to match their level of financial literacy ensures effective communication and engagement.

- Family Dynamics: Within families, consider the different financial knowledge levels and tailor the information accordingly. This might involve simplifying concepts for children or addressing specific financial concerns for different family members.

- Community Outreach: When sharing financial knowledge in a community setting, consider the unique challenges and opportunities within that community. Understanding local economic conditions and cultural factors enhances the relevance of the information shared.

3. Foundational Financial Concepts:

- Budgeting: Start with foundational concepts like budgeting. Teach individuals how to create and maintain a budget to manage income, expenses, and savings effectively.

- Savings and Emergency Funds: Emphasize the importance of savings and building emergency funds. Discuss the role of emergency funds in providing financial stability during unexpected situations.

- Debt Management: Address the basics of debt, including different types of debt, interest rates, and strategies for managing and reducing debt. Teach the importance of responsible borrowing and the long-term impact of debt on financial health.

4. Interactive Learning:

- Simulations and Games: Engage learners through financial simulations and games. Interactive experiences can make complex financial concepts more digestible and enjoyable, especially for younger audiences.

- Real-Life Scenarios: Share real-life financial scenarios and case studies. Analyzing actual situations helps individuals connect theoretical concepts to practical decision-making.

- Role-Playing Exercises: Conduct role-playing exercises to simulate financial decision-making. This approach allows participants to experience the consequences of different choices in a controlled environment.

5. Utilizing Technology:

- Online Resources: Leverage online resources and educational platforms. There are numerous websites, apps, and courses that offer interactive financial education materials for various age groups and knowledge levels.

- Webinars and Workshops: Conduct webinars or workshops to reach a wider audience. Virtual sessions provide flexibility and accessibility for individuals seeking financial education.

- Financial Apps: Introduce individuals to financial apps that can assist with budgeting, tracking expenses, and managing investments. Familiarizing them with these tools enhances their ability to navigate the digital financial landscape.

6. Teaching Long-Term Investing:

- Compound Interest: Explain the concept of compound interest and its role in long-term investing. Demonstrating how regular contributions can grow over time highlights the power of compounding.

- Diversification: Teach the importance of diversifying investments to manage risk. Emphasize how a well-balanced portfolio can weather market fluctuations more effectively.

- Retirement Planning: Discuss the significance of early retirement planning. Introduce retirement accounts, employer-sponsored plans, and the impact of consistent contributions over a working career.

7. Encouraging Financial Responsibility:

- Ethical Financial Behavior: Emphasize the importance of ethical financial behavior. Instill values of honesty, integrity, and responsible financial decision-making to foster a culture of financial responsibility.

- Environmental and Social Considerations: Discuss the growing importance of considering environmental, social, and governance (ESG) factors in financial decision-making. Encourage socially responsible investing and consumption.

- Philanthropy and Giving Back: Introduce the concept of philanthropy and giving back to the community. Teach individuals how financial success can be leveraged to contribute positively to society.

8. Addressing Behavioral Finance:

- Understanding Behavioral Biases: Explore behavioral biases that can impact financial decisions. Discuss concepts like loss aversion, overconfidence, and herd mentality to help individuals recognize and manage these biases.

- Goal Visualization: Encourage individuals to visualize their financial goals. Creating a clear picture of desired outcomes enhances motivation and helps overcome behavioral barriers to financial success.

- Mindful Spending: Discuss the importance of mindful spending. Encourage individuals to align their spending with their values and long-term financial objectives.

9. Navigating Economic Challenges:

- Preparing for Economic Downturns: Educate individuals on preparing for economic downturns. Discuss the importance of emergency funds, debt reduction, and strategic financial planning during challenging economic times.

- Adapting to Technological Changes: Acknowledge the impact of technological advancements on financial landscapes. Help individuals navigate digital currencies, online banking, and emerging financial technologies.

10. Measuring Success:

- Financial Health Metrics: Introduce financial health metrics. These may include credit scores, debt-to-income ratios, and net worth calculations. Regularly tracking these metrics allows individuals to gauge their financial progress.

- Goal Achievement: Celebrate goal achievements. Recognizing and celebrating milestones, whether it's paying off a debt or reaching a savings target, reinforces positive financial behaviors.

- Feedback and Adjustments: Encourage feedback and adjustments to financial plans. Financial situations and goals may evolve, and a willingness to adapt strategies based on feedback ensures ongoing success.

Passing on financial knowledge is an investment in individual and collective prosperity. By tailoring approaches to diverse audiences, utilizing interactive learning methods, and addressing both foundational and advanced financial concepts, educators can create a positive and lasting impact. The goal is not only to equip individuals with the skills to navigate their personal finances successfully but also to contribute to a society where financial literacy is widespread, empowering everyone to make informed and responsible financial decisions.

Through effective financial education, we can build a future where financial well-being is accessible to all, fostering economic resilience and stability.

Creating a legacy of financial empowerment is a powerful and enduring gift that transcends generations. It involves not only securing personal financial success but also imparting knowledge, values, and skills that empower family members and communities to thrive economically. This guide explores the principles and actions needed to establish a lasting legacy of financial empowerment.

1. Building Wealth with Purpose:

- Setting a Vision: A legacy of financial empowerment begins with a clear vision. Define overarching financial goals that go beyond personal wealth accumulation and encompass the well-being of future generations and the broader community.

- Integrating Values: Infuse values into financial decisions. Consider ethical investing, sustainable practices, and philanthropy as integral parts of wealth-building, ensuring that financial success aligns with broader social and environmental goals.

- Generational Inclusivity: Extend financial planning discussions to include multiple generations. Inclusivity ensures that younger family members are educated about financial principles and actively involved in shaping the family's financial legacy.

2. Educational Foundations:

- Financial Literacy Initiatives: Implement financial literacy initiatives within the family. Establish regular educational sessions covering topics such as budgeting, investing, debt management, and ethical financial behavior.

- Formal Education: Encourage formal financial education. Support family members in pursuing relevant courses, certifications, or degrees in finance, economics, or business, fostering a deep understanding of financial principles.

- Mentorship Programs: Create mentorship programs within the family. Pair experienced family members with younger individuals to provide guidance, share experiences, and offer insights into financial decision-making.

3. Practical Money Management:

- Budgeting Practices: Instill strong budgeting practices. Teach family members the importance of creating and sticking to a budget, emphasizing the value of disciplined spending and saving.

- Emergency Fund Culture: Cultivate a culture of emergency fund preparedness. Emphasize the significance of having an emergency fund to navigate unexpected financial challenges without jeopardizing long-term financial goals.

- Debt Management Strategies: Share effective debt management strategies. Guide family members on responsible borrowing, debt reduction techniques, and the long-term impact of interest rates on financial well-being.

4. Legacy Planning:

- Estate Planning: Engage in comprehensive estate planning. Establish wills, trusts, and other legal structures to ensure a smooth transfer of assets and wealth. Include provisions for charitable giving to contribute positively to the community.

- Communication of Values: Clearly communicate family values through the estate planning process. This ensures that future generations understand the purpose behind the family's wealth and are equipped to continue the legacy of financial empowerment.

- Succession Planning: Develop a succession plan for family businesses or financial leadership roles. This involves identifying and preparing successors, ensuring a seamless transition of responsibilities and preserving the family's financial legacy.

5. Philanthropic Endeavors:

- Community Engagement: Actively engage in philanthropy. Encourage family members to participate in community service, charitable initiatives, or impact investing to address social issues and contribute to the betterment of society.

- Establishing Foundations: Consider establishing family foundations. These entities can serve as a vehicle for strategic philanthropy, allowing the family to support causes aligned with their values and create a lasting positive impact.

- Educational Scholarships: Create educational scholarships for family members and community members. Investing in education enables individuals to break barriers and enhances their ability to achieve financial success.

6. Entrepreneurial Empowerment:

- Supporting Entrepreneurship: Encourage entrepreneurial endeavors within the family. Provide mentorship, financial support, and guidance for family members seeking to start their own businesses, fostering innovation and economic independence.

- Investing in Ventures: Explore opportunities to invest in family members' business ventures. This not only supports entrepreneurship but also aligns financial resources with the family's commitment to economic empowerment.

- Business Education: Offer business education opportunities. Whether through workshops, seminars, or formal education, providing resources for family members to enhance their business acumen contributes to long-term financial success.

7. Investment Strategies:

- Sustainable and Responsible Investing: Embrace sustainable and responsible investing. Align investment portfolios with environmental, social, and governance (ESG) principles, contributing to positive societal and environmental outcomes.

- Diversification and Risk Management: Instill the importance of diversification and risk management in investment strategies. Educate family members on balancing risk and reward, adjusting portfolios based on changing market conditions, and maintaining a long-term perspective.

- Impact Investing: Explore impact investing opportunities. Direct investments toward projects and companies that not only offer financial returns but also contribute to positive social or environmental change.

8. Cultivating a Mindset of Abundance:

- Positive Money Mindset: Foster a mindset of abundance within the family. Encourage optimism, creativity, and a belief that opportunities for financial success are abundant, leading to a proactive approach to wealth-building.

- Financial Goal Setting: Guide family members in setting ambitious yet achievable financial goals. Establishing a culture of goal setting instills a sense of purpose and direction, motivating individuals to strive for continuous improvement.

- Resilience in Adversity: Teach resilience in the face of financial challenges. Acknowledge that setbacks may occur, but emphasize the importance of learning from adversity, adapting strategies, and maintaining a long-term perspective.

9. Communication and Transparency:

- Open Financial Discussions: Foster open and transparent communication about finances within the family. Create a culture where family members feel comfortable discussing financial goals, challenges, and aspirations.

- Financial Meetings: Schedule regular family financial meetings. These gatherings provide opportunities to review financial plans, share updates on investments, and ensure that everyone is aligned with the family's financial vision.

- Financial Transparency: Emphasize the importance of financial transparency. Share information about the family's financial situation, including assets, investments, and philanthropic activities, to promote a sense of shared responsibility.

10. Leading by Example:

- Demonstrating Responsible Behavior: Lead by example in demonstrating responsible financial behavior. Whether through prudent spending, disciplined saving, or ethical investing, exemplify the values and practices that define the family's financial legacy.

- Continuous Learning: Embrace a culture of continuous learning. Stay informed about evolving financial trends, investment strategies, and economic developments, setting an example for family members to prioritize ongoing education.

- Adapting to Change: Demonstrate adaptability to change. Economic landscapes, financial markets, and family dynamics evolve over time. Modeling the ability to adapt strategies and embrace change instills resilience in future generations.

Creating a legacy of financial empowerment involves a holistic approach that extends beyond individual wealth accumulation. It requires intentional efforts to impart financial knowledge, instill values, and actively contribute to the well-being of future generations and the broader community. By focusing on education, philanthropy, entrepreneurship, and responsible investing, families can establish a legacy that not only endures but positively shapes the economic landscape for years to come. Through these intentional actions, a family's financial legacy becomes a beacon of empowerment, inspiring others to pursue financial success with purpose and integrity.

CONCLUSION

In the exploration of creating a legacy of financial empowerment, several key concepts emerge that form the foundation for a lasting impact. From building wealth with purpose to imparting financial knowledge and fostering a mindset of abundance, these concepts collectively contribute to a holistic approach to financial empowerment. Let's recap these essential elements, each playing a crucial role in creating a legacy that transcends generations.

- Building Wealth with Purpose:
The journey toward financial empowerment starts with a clear vision and purpose. It involves setting overarching financial goals that extend beyond personal wealth accumulation. By integrating values into financial decisions, individuals can align their financial success with broader social and environmental goals, creating a purpose-driven approach to wealth-building.

- Generational Inclusivity:
A sustainable financial legacy includes multiple generations. Engaging younger family members in

financial discussions and decisions ensures the transfer of knowledge and values. This inclusivity sets the stage for a collaborative approach to managing family wealth, fostering a sense of shared responsibility and commitment to financial empowerment.

- Educational Foundations:
Financial education forms the bedrock of a legacy of financial empowerment. From basic financial literacy initiatives within the family to formal education in finance, economics, or business, imparting knowledge equips family members with the skills to make informed decisions and navigate the complexities of the financial landscape.

- Practical Money Management:
Sound money management practices are essential for sustainable financial empowerment. This includes instilling strong budgeting practices, cultivating a culture of emergency fund preparedness, and teaching effective debt management strategies. Practical money management ensures a solid foundation for financial stability and growth.

- Legacy Planning:
Comprehensive legacy planning is crucial for ensuring a smooth transfer of assets and values across generations. Estate planning, clear communication of family values, and succession planning for family businesses are integral components. This strategic approach lays the groundwork for preserving and perpetuating the family's financial legacy.

- Philanthropic Endeavors:
Contributing to the well-being of the community through philanthropy is a hallmark of a meaningful financial legacy. Engaging in community service, establishing family foundations, and creating educational scholarships are ways to positively impact society and instill the value of giving back in future generations.

- Entrepreneurial Empowerment:
Encouraging entrepreneurial endeavors within the family fosters innovation and economic independence. Supporting family members in starting businesses, providing mentorship, and investing in entrepreneurial ventures contribute to a

legacy that champions creativity and
self-sufficiency.

- Investment Strategies:
Strategic investment choices play a pivotal role in a
legacy of financial empowerment. Embracing
sustainable and responsible investing, diversifying
portfolios, and exploring impact investing
opportunities align financial resources with ethical
principles and contribute to positive societal and
environmental outcomes.

- Cultivating a Mindset of Abundance:
Fostering a mindset of abundance is key to creating
a positive and proactive approach to
wealth-building. Emphasizing a positive money
mindset, setting ambitious yet achievable financial
goals, and promoting resilience in the face of
challenges contribute to a culture of continuous
improvement and success.

- Communication and Transparency:
Open and transparent communication about finances
within the family is essential. Regular family
financial meetings, financial transparency, and
creating a culture where family members feel

comfortable discussing financial matters build trust and ensure everyone is aligned with the family's financial vision.

- Leading by Example:
Leading by example is a powerful way to shape a financial legacy. Demonstrating responsible financial behavior, embracing continuous learning, and adapting to change model the values and practices that define the family's commitment to financial empowerment. This exemplary leadership sets the tone for future generations.

In the pursuit of creating a legacy of financial empowerment, these key concepts collectively form a comprehensive framework. From setting a purpose-driven vision and fostering inclusivity across generations to embracing sustainable investments and philanthropy, each concept contributes to a legacy that goes beyond wealth accumulation. By intentionally integrating these elements into financial planning and decision-making, individuals and families can build a legacy that not only endures but positively impacts the well-being of future generations and the broader community. This holistic approach ensures that the legacy of financial empowerment becomes a guiding light, inspiring others to pursue financial success with purpose, integrity, and a commitment to positive change.

Sustained financial empowerment is a journey that demands dedication, resilience, and a long-term perspective. Navigating the complexities of personal finance requires a steadfast commitment to the principles of financial empowerment. Here's an encouraging guide to foster sustained financial empowerment, encompassing key principles, mindset shifts, and practical strategies for enduring success.

Embrace the Journey: Financial empowerment is a journey, not a destination. Recognize that achieving lasting financial success takes time and effort. Celebrate small victories, understand setbacks are natural, and commit to continuous improvement.

Define Your Why: Clearly define financial goals and the reasons behind them. Having a purpose-driven approach strengthens your resolve to make sound financial decisions.

Cultivate a Positive Money Mindset: Shift from scarcity to abundance. Cultivate gratitude, focus on possibilities, and approach financial challenges as opportunities for growth and learning.

Set Realistic and Achievable Goals: Establish clear, realistic, and achievable financial goals. Break down larger objectives into smaller, manageable steps, celebrating each milestone along the way.

Budget Wisely: Craft a well-defined budget as a powerful tool for managing income, expenses, and savings. Regularly review and adjust to align with financial goals and changing circumstances.

Build and Maintain an Emergency Fund: Financial resilience is key. Maintain an emergency fund to cover unexpected expenses and prevent dipping into long-term savings during challenging times.

Educate Yourself Continuously: Commit to continuous education about personal finance, investments, and economic trends for informed decision-making.

Invest for the Long Term: Adopt a long-term perspective in your investment strategy, focusing on diversification, risk management, and regular contributions to your portfolio.

Diversify Your Income Streams: Explore opportunities to diversify income sources, enhancing financial stability and wealth accumulation.

Manage Debt Responsibly: Develop a responsible approach to borrowing, prioritize high-interest debt repayment, and avoid unnecessary liabilities.

Practice Mindful Spending: Align expenses with values and priorities, enhancing financial awareness and supporting sustained empowerment.

Prioritize Financial Wellness: View financial empowerment as integral to overall well-being. Prioritize self-care and mental health for sound financial decisions.

Build a Support System: Surround yourself with a supportive network to provide encouragement, accountability, and valuable insights.

Adapt to Change: Flexibility and adaptability are crucial. Embrace change, adjust strategies, and approach challenges as opportunities for growth.

Celebrate Your Progress: Acknowledge and celebrate financial achievements, reinforcing positive behaviors and sustaining motivation.

Contribute to Others: Sharing financial success through philanthropy, mentorship, or community initiatives fosters a sense of fulfillment and motivation.

Reflect and Reframe: Regularly reflect on the financial journey, learn from experiences, and reframe setbacks as opportunities for growth.

Seek Professional Guidance: Consider seeking professional financial advice for tailored insights and strategies.

Practice Gratitude: Cultivate a mindset of gratitude, acknowledging progress and focusing on the positive aspects of your financial life.

Remember Your Impact: Recognize that financial decisions have a lasting impact on your life and future generations. Commit to sound financial principles, shaping a positive ripple effect.

In conclusion, sustained financial empowerment is a holistic endeavor involving mindset, habits, and strategic actions. Embrace the journey, stay focused, and adapt to change for enduring success. Your commitment goes beyond individual prosperity, shaping a legacy that positively influences others and future generations. Stay encouraged, resilient, and advance toward lasting financial empowerment.

Appendices

Additional Resources

Here are some additional resources to further support your journey toward financial empowerment:

Books:

1. "The Total Money Makeover" by Dave Ramsey: A practical guide to managing money and eliminating debt.

2. "Your Money or Your Life" by Vicki Robin and Joe Dominguez:Explores the relationship between money and life, offering insights on financial independence.

3. "Rich Dad Poor Dad" by Robert T. Kiyosaki: Challenges conventional beliefs about money and provides principles for building wealth.

4. "The Millionaire Next Door" by Thomas J. Stanley and William D. Danko: Examines the habits

of millionaires and offers insights on accumulating wealth.

Websites and Blogs:

1. Investopedia (www.investopedia.com):A comprehensive resource for financial education, covering topics from investing to personal finance.

2. The Motley Fool (www.fool.com):Provides investment insights, advice, and educational content for investors.

3. NerdWallet (www.nerdwallet.com):Offers tools and resources for budgeting, investing, and making informed financial decisions.

4. Khan Academy (www.khanacademy.org):Provides free online courses in various subjects, including finance and economics.

Podcasts:

1. "The Dave Ramsey Show":Dave Ramsey offers practical financial advice and answers listener questions.

2. "BiggerPockets Money Podcast":Focuses on real estate and financial independence, featuring interviews with successful investors.

3. "Afford Anything Podcast" with Paula Pant:Explores financial independence, investing, and lifestyle design.

Apps:

1. YNAB (You Need A Budget): A budgeting app that helps users gain control of their finances and prioritize spending.

2. Mint: A personal finance app that tracks spending, creates budgets, and provides insights into financial habits.

3. Acorns: An app that rounds up everyday purchases to invest spare change in a diversified portfolio.

Online Courses:

1. Coursera (www.coursera.org):Offers a variety of finance-related courses from top universities and institutions.

2. Udemy (www.udemy.com):Provides affordable online courses on personal finance, investing, and other financial topics.

Financial Planning Tools:

1. Personal Capital:A financial management tool that offers budgeting, investment tracking, and retirement planning.

2. SmartAsset (www.smartasset.com):Provides tools and calculators to help with mortgage decisions, retirement planning, and more.

Remember to explore these resources based on your specific needs and interests. Each person's financial journey is unique, and these tools can provide valuable guidance along the way.

Practical Application Guide

Practical application is key to implementing financial empowerment strategies. Here are some worksheets and tools that you can use to actively apply financial principles to your personal situation:

1. Budgeting Worksheet:

- Description: A detailed budgeting worksheet to help you track income, expenses, and savings. This sheet includes categories such as housing, utilities, groceries, entertainment, and more.

- Purpose: To create a realistic budget and gain a clear understanding of where your money is going.

- Tool: [Budgeting Worksheet](https://www.vertex42.com/ExcelTempla tes/personal-budget-spreadsheet.html)

2. Emergency Fund Calculator:

- Description: A calculator to determine how much you need in your emergency fund based on your monthly expenses.

- Purpose: To establish and maintain an emergency fund that provides financial security in unexpected situations.

- Tool: [Emergency Fund Calculator](https://www.nerdwallet.com/personal-finance/emergency-fund-calculator)

3. Debt Payoff Planner:

- Description: A tool to create a debt payoff plan, considering multiple debts, interest rates, and payoff strategies.

- Purpose: To systematically reduce and eliminate debt, improving overall financial health.

- Tool: [Debt Payoff Calculator](https://www.nerdwallet.com/article/finance/debt-payoff-calculator)

4. Investment Portfolio Tracker:

- Description: A spreadsheet to track and manage your investment portfolio, including stocks, bonds, and other investments.

- Purpose: To monitor the performance of your investments and ensure alignment with your financial goals.

- Tool: [Investment Portfolio Tracker](https://www.microsoft.com/en-us/templates/investment-portfolio-tracker-TC010210607)

 5. Income and Expense Tracker:

- Description: A simple tool to record your monthly income and expenses, helping you identify areas for potential savings.

- Purpose: To gain a clear overview of your financial inflows and outflows.

- Tool: [Income and Expense Tracker](https://templates.office.com/en-us/income-and-expense-tracker-tm16401276)

6. Financial Goal Setting Worksheet:

- Description: A worksheet to define and prioritize your financial goals, including short-term and long-term objectives.

- Purpose: To establish clear, achievable financial goals that align with your values.

- Tool: [Financial Goal Setting Worksheet](https://www.schwabmoneywise.com/public/file/p-960-Worksheet-Setting-Financial-Goals.pdf)

7. Savings Challenge Tracker:

- Description: A tracker for popular savings challenges, such as the 52-week savings challenge or monthly savings goals.

- Purpose: To make saving money more engaging and manageable with incremental challenges.

- Tool: [Savings Challenge Tracker](https://www.thebalance.com/52-week-money-saving-challenge-2890251)

8. Net Worth Calculator:

- Description: A calculator to determine your net worth by subtracting your liabilities from your assets.

- Purpose: To measure your overall financial progress and assess your financial health.

- Tool: [Net Worth Calculator](https://www.nerdwallet.com/personal-finance/net-worth-calculator)

9. Retirement Planning Worksheet:

- Description: A worksheet to estimate your retirement needs, taking into account factors like current savings, expected Social Security benefits, and future expenses.

- Purpose: To develop a strategy for building a retirement nest egg that aligns with your lifestyle goals.

- Tool: [Retirement Planning
Worksheet](https://www.schwabmoneywise.com/pu
blic/file/p-694-Savings-and-Retirement-Worksheet.p
df)

10. Financial Education Resources:

- Description:A curated list of online courses, books,
and websites for ongoing financial education.

- Purpose:To facilitate continuous learning and stay
informed about evolving financial trends.

- Tool: [Financial Education
Resources](https://www.consumerfinance.gov/practi
tioner-resources/financial-education/resources/)

Feel free to customize these tools according to your
specific needs and preferences. Regularly revisiting
and updating these worksheets will contribute to the
ongoing success of your financial empowerment
journey.

Financial Empowerment Action Plan Worksheet

Goal Setting:
1. Short-Term Goals (Next 6 Months):
  - Identify specific financial goals you aim to achieve in the next six months.

2. Mid-Term Goals (6 Months to 2 Years):
  - Define financial milestones you plan to reach within the next two years.

3. Long-Term Goals (Beyond 2 Years):
  - Outline your overarching financial aspirations for the long term.

Budgeting and Spending:
4. Monthly Budget:
  - Create a detailed monthly budget that includes all sources of income and itemized expenses.

5. Mindful Spending Reflection:
  - Reflect on your recent spending habits and identify areas where you can practice more mindful spending aligned with your values.

Emergency Fund:
6. Emergency Fund Calculation:
  - Use the emergency fund calculator to determine the appropriate size for your emergency fund based on your monthly expenses.

7. Emergency Fund Progress Tracker:
  - Track your progress in building and maintaining your emergency fund over time.

Debt Management:
8. Debt Payoff Plan:
  - List all your debts, including amounts and interest rates, and outline a strategic debt payoff plan.

Investment and Net Worth:
9. Investment Portfolio Snapshot:
  - Create a snapshot of your current investment portfolio, including types of investments and current values.

10. Net Worth Calculation:
  - Calculate your net worth by listing your assets and liabilities.

Financial Education:

11. Continuous Learning Plan:

   - Develop a plan for continuous financial education, including books, online courses, and other resources you intend to explore.

Reflection and Celebration:

12. Celebrate Small Victories:

   - Acknowledge and celebrate recent financial achievements or progress.

Action Steps:

13. Next Steps:

   - Outline specific action steps based on your reflections and the goals you've set. What will you do in the next month to move closer to your financial aspirations?

Readers are encouraged to use this worksheet actively as they progress through the book. Regularly revisiting and updating it will help them stay focused on their financial goals and track their journey toward sustained financial empowerment.

Monthly Budgeting Worksheet

Income:
1. Salary: $___________
2. Additional Income: $___________ (e.g., bonuses, side hustle)

Necessities:
1. Rent/Mortgage: $___________
2. Utilities: $___________
3. Insurance: $___________
4. Groceries: $___________
5. Transportation: $___________
6. Other Essentials: $___________ (e.g., healthcare, childcare)

Discretionary Spending:
1. Dining Out: $___________
2. Entertainment: $___________
3. Shopping: $___________
4. Hobbies/Activities: $___________
5. Miscellaneous: $___________

Savings and Goals:
1. Emergency Fund: $___________

2. Retirement Savings: $____________
3. Other Goals: $____________ (e.g., vacation, home
purchase)

Total Income: $____________

Total Expenses: $____________

Remaining (Income - Expenses): $____________

How to Use:
1. Fill in your estimated monthly income for each
category.
2. Allocate percentages or dollar amounts to each
expense category.
3. As the month progresses, record your actual
spending in each category.
4. Compare actual spending to the budget regularly.
5. Make adjustments as needed to stay within your
financial goals.

Tips:
- Aim to allocate a portion of your income to
savings and financial goals.

- Regularly review and adjust your budget based on changing circumstances.
- Use budgeting apps for seamless tracking and categorization.